The Library of the China-Africa Institute

Research Institutions on African Studies in China

Edited by
Zhan Shiming

中国社会科学出版社
CHINA SOCIAL SCIENCES PRESS

图书在版编目（CIP）数据

中国的非洲研究机构 = Research Institutions on African Studies in China : 英文 / 詹世明编 . -- 北京 : 中国社会科学出版社 , 2021.11

（中国非洲研究院文库）

ISBN 978-7-5203-9362-1

Ⅰ．①中… Ⅱ．①詹… Ⅲ．①非洲—研究机构—概况—英文 Ⅳ．① D74-24

中国版本图书馆 CIP 数据核字 (2021) 第 239227 号

出 版 人　赵剑英
责任编辑　姜阿平　高　俐
责任校对　夏　侠
责任印制　张雪娇

出　　版　中国社会科学出版社
社　　址　北京鼓楼西大街甲 158 号
邮　　编　100720
网　　址　http://www.csspw.cn
发 行 部　010－84083685
门 市 部　010－84029450
经　　销　新华书店及其他书店

印　　刷　北京君升印刷有限公司
装　　订　廊坊市广阳区广增装订厂
版　　次　2021 年 11 月第 1 版
印　　次　2021 年 11 月第 1 次印刷

开　　本　710×1000　1/16
印　　张　13.25
插　　页　2
字　　数　209 千字
定　　价　88.00 元

凡购买中国社会科学出版社图书，如有质量问题请与本社营销中心联系调换
电话：010－84083683

Preface

This book provides a list of National Societies on African Studies in China, and Other Research Organizations on African Studies in China. In order to reflect the geographical distribution of China's research institutions on African studies to a certain extent, Other Research Organizations on African Studies in China (including those from the party, government and military systems, those in the institutions of higher learning, and those under the Chinese Academy of Social Sciences, as well as non-governmental think tanks) are listed in the order of Chinese phonetics according to the initials of the provinces, autonomous regions, or municipalities where the Organizations are located (and the Organizations located in the same province or municipality are listed in the order of the time of their establishment). To ensure information accuracy, all the introductions are provided by the research institutions themselves, with only necessary changes made during editing.

Contents

African Studies in China: Retrospect and Prospect

Li Anshan

China's systematic understanding and research of Africa began since the establishment of People's Republic of China, which can be roughly divided into three stages. Supporting Africa (1950-1965). Political emphasis determined that the contact with and study on Africa should be based on support for national independence movements. Understanding Africa (1966-1976). Some institutions translated a large number of works in the "Cultural Revolution" to enhance understanding of Africa. Studying Africa (1977-). The Reform and Opening up prompted the academic community to become familiar with Africa and start preliminary research. The development of China Africa relations has promoted all-round research on Africa. This article attempts to further explore China's African studies, which are divided into five parts, a historical background of relationship between China and Africa, a brief illustration of the achievements of four generations (especially young people) of scholars, the participation and contribution of Chinese scholars in the international academia; the development of research institutions, and an analysis of the new trend of African studies in China.

China-African Relations: History and Present

China-Africa relations began in ancient times. "Silk Road" existed since the Han Dynasty (202 B.C.-220 A.D.). In 1993, Austrian archeologists discovered the fiber of worm-silk in the hair of a female corpse of the 21st Dynasty (1070-945.B.C.) in Egypt. Since only China had the technology of producing silk at the time, the product was most probably made in China and transported to Egypt.[1] According to Sun, there are two ways—the North Way and the South Way to connect China and the "West".[2] The "North Way", from Chang'an to Sogdiana, through the border between the Parthian Empire and the Roman Empire, by water to, Damascus and Gaza, finally reached what is now known as Alexandria in Egypt. This was the main trade route from China to Egypt. The "South Way", stretched from Loulan to today's Kabul, and then southward to the upper reaches of the Sindhu River, then to the port of Karachi, finally reaching the countries along the Indian Ocean and in further west. There were other connections between China and Africa as well.

Besides the land route, there was the Maritime Silk Road. Historically, various ports along the East African coast and in west Indian Ocean were important destinations for maritime traffic between China and Africa, or middle stations for Chinese vessels to go further to Europe. According to historical records, the names of Ethiopia, Somalia, Kenya, Tanzania, Mozambique, Madagascar and other countries all appeared in various travel notes and official history of ancient China. China's maritime contact with Africa, especially East Africa, was much earlier than Da Gama's voyage around the Cape of Good Hope to East Africa. Cities in Africa did act as ports, supply depots, settlements and protection areas in China's maritime endeavor in ancient time.

At present, the BRI tries to link the world with capital, trade and personnel. Africa can play an even more important role. It is found that the BRI is constantly making with African countries gradually involved. At first, the only African country included in the proposed 65 countries of the BRI was Egypt. Later, the Chinese official mentioned African countries as a "natural extension" of One Belt One Road (OBOR). During his visit to Madagascar, Foreign Minister Wang Yi proposed that "both countries seize the two major opportunities for international

1 "Egypt used Chinese silk 3000 years ago", April 2, 1993, *People's Daily*.

2 "West" in ancient China indicates the foreign land west of China, including Mid-Asia and West Asia, North Africa and further westwards (Sun, 1979).

cooperation respectively brought about by the implementation of the outcome of the 2015 Forum on China-Africa Cooperation in Johannesburg and the promotion of international cooperation under the Belt and Road Initiative".[1] This invitation was confirmed when President Xi Jinping met Madagascar President HeryRajaonarimampianina and both countries signed the "Maritime Road Memorandum of the Understanding".[2] Till now, 37 African countries have signed the MOU or agreement of the BRI with China.[3]

Yet what is the role that Africa can play in the BRI? In general, ports on the east coast of Africa are a key part of the Maritime Silk Road. African islands in the West Indian Ocean constitute an expressive fulcrum of maritime traffic. Maritime safety in the Gulf of Aden is an important guarantee for the international sea route, Africa is becoming an important investment and trade partner of Asian countries, and it is an important hub and transshipment point for maritime exchanges between Asia and Europe. BRI is supposed to bring mutual benefits to both China and the partners. China has gained a great deal from Africa, such as political support and economic benefits, and vice versa. There are examples of bilateral cooperation with Ethiopia, Kenya, Tanzania, etc., such as Chinese Light Rail in Addis Ababa of Ethiopia, first batch of Kenyan female drivers in Mombasa-Nairobi Railway, the Chinese-built Dar es Salaam University Library, etc. All these projects symbolize the concrete result of cooperation related to the BRI in Africa. In addition, there is a great deal of similarity between Chinese and African civilizations and both sides can learn from each other in many aspects. That is why mutual understanding/learning is very important for both sides, thus African

---

1 "Chinese FM meets Madagascar's president on cooperation under Belt-Road Initiative", January 8, 2017, Xinhaunet. http://www.xinhuanet.com//english/2017-01/08/c_135964672.htm. Accessed 2019-4-3.

2 "Xi meets Madagascar's president", September 5, 2018, *China Daily*. http://www.chinadaily.com.cn/a/201809/05/WS5b8f67a7a31033b4f46545dd.html. Accessed 2019-4-3.

3 "China signed BRI Memorandum with 37 African countries and AU", September 7, 2018. Chinese Government Net. http://www.gov.cn/xinwen/2018-09/08/content_5320263.htm. Accessed 2019-4-3.

study becomes a vital factor in promoting bilateral relations and facilitating the implementation of the BRI.

African Studies in China: Four Generations

China's African study has gone through the efforts of four generations. Two of my articles have explored China's African studies in the 20th and 21st century. Here is a brief survey of the achievements of the four generations.

China's African study began with a focus on Egypt. Duanfang (1861-1911), an epigraphist in the late Qing Dynasty, collected Egyptian antiquities. Huang Junsheng and Li Dongfang studied Egyptian characters in the early 20th century. Xia Nai, the "father of Chinese Egyptology", mastered hieroglyphs and participated in the archaeological excavation in Egypt while studying in London. He was appointed "Academician" by seven conntries. At the beginning of the 20th Century, Chinese scholars began to study the early Sino-African exchanges. The understanding and systematic study of Africa itself began with the establishment of the People's Republic of China. The first generation (1950s-1970s) includes Zhang Tiesheng, Yang Renpian, Ma Jian, Na Zhong and Zhang Tongzhu. Zhang Tiesheng (1904-1979) was the first leader of the Institute of West-Asia and Africa (hereafter IWAAS) of the Chinese Academy of Social Sciences (hereafter CASS), formerly under the Section of Philosophy and Social Sciences of the Chinese Academy of Sciences, and he published a book on China Africa relations. Yang Renpian (1903-1973) of Peking University graduated from Oxford University majoring in French history,changed his field to African history in 1958 and mentored younger scholars. His work were later collated and published by his students. Ma Jian did his study in Egypt in the 1930s and his translation of Koran was regarded as the official version in China. Na Zhong (1909-2008) of Beijing Foreign Studies University graduated from Azhar University in Egypt in 1940.

He studied the history of Egypt and Arab all his life. He was the president of the Chinese Society of African Historical Studies.[1] Zhang Tongzhu (1915-2008) of Nanjing University established the African Geography Research Office in 1965 and coordinated the national project "Strategic study on African Economic and Social Development" and the research on African economic development.[2] Although Professor Zhou Yiliang didn't specialize in African history, yet he discussed the history of China-Africa relations in a Ghanaian journal.

The second generation was from the 1980s to the end of the 20th century. Since the Reform and Opening up, scholars have gained unprecedented opportunities. This generation includes university professors and researchers from different institutions. For example, Ge Ji, Zhao Guozhong, Tu Erkang, Chen Gongyuan, Wu Bingzhen, Yang Lihua, Xu Jiming, Gao Jinyuan, Wu Qiyang, Tang Dadun of the Institute of West Asia and Africa, Yang Haocheng and Peng Kunyuan of the Institute of World History, Ge Gongshang of the Institute of Ethnology and Anthropology (All above in CASS), Xia Jisheng, ZhengJiaxin, Lu Ting'en, He Fangchuan and Ning Sao of Peking University, Zhang Wenchun of Beijing Normal University, Zeng Zungu, Su Shirong and Jiang Zhongjin of Nanjing University, AI Zhouchang of East China Normal University, Gu Zhangyi of Minzu University of China, Li Guangyi of Xiangtan University, Zhao Shuhui of Renmin University, Shen Fuwei of Suzhou University, Xu Yongzhang of Zhengzhou University, Zhang Xiang of Nankai University. Liu Wenpeng of Inner Mongolia University for Nationalities has trained a number of scholars for Chinese Egyptology. Gao Jinyuan, He Fangchuan, Ge Ji, Yang Lihua and other scholars published articles in English. The achievements of this generation include three aspects. Institutional Construction: The Chinese Association of African Studies

1 "Professor Na Zhong", September 15, 2011. http://www.chinadaily.com.cn/dfpd/bw70/2011-09/15/content_13695495.htm.

2 Wu Nan, "Academicians memorized the hundredth anniversary of Mr. Zhang Tongzhu", December 1, 2015. http://news.nju.edu.cn/show_article_2_40480.

was established in 1979, and the Chinese Society of African Historical Studies in 1980. Organizational work: They organized various meetings of African scholars from different institutions and universities, coordinating debates and research on various issues. Academic achievements: They published research works, especially the "African Studies" series and some reference books,[1]In addition, the translation of various African books and the UNESCO General History of Africa (1-8 volumes). Some of them continue to be used in the 21st century.

The establishment of the Forum on China-Africa cooperation (FOCAC) ushered in a new era of African studies in China. The cooperation between China and Africa needs the support of the academia, which must also meet the requirements of the government, the business community and the public. The third generation of scholars have received formal academic training and they have more opportunities to visit Africa than their predecessors, receiving education or training abroad, and gradually engaged in the international academia. The importance that the nation attached to academic research has provided various funds and favorable conditions, thus promotes the academic community to pay attention to research topics related to Africa. ShuYunguo, Yang Guang, Zhang Hongming, Li Xinfeng, Liu Qinjian, Liu Hongwu, Yan Haiying, Jin Shoufu, Mu Tao, Zhang Zhongxiang and Zhu Zhenwu, etc., have successively undertaken or participated in major national research projects on African history, China's African strategy, EU's aid to Africa, history of China-Africa relations, China Africa cooperation and African literature. They are deepening their research on Africa. Take the project "African Economic History" as an example. On one hand, it is recognized that the research level of China's African economic history is not high compared to that of foreign countries, "so it is difficult for China's version of African economic history to catch up with the world's cutting-edge level in the overall research level"; on

1 The most prominent is the publication of three volumes of *General History of Africa* (1996), GeJie, ed. *Concise Encyclopaedia of Sub-Saharan Africa* (2000) andZhaoGuozhong, ed., *Concise Encyclopaedia of West Asia and North Africa (Middle East)* (2000).

the other hand, "China's version of African economic history still has its own characteristics, Such as making full use of Chinese ancient books and materials, comprehensively and in-depth elaboration of China-Africa economic and trade relations and unique historical stages of African economic history". African languages are taught in many universities. The publication of various works and translations has opened up readers' horizons, and the construction of African country studies and think-tanks are a good try. African research institutions have various publications, thus contributed to the popularization and deepening of African research. They have strengthened closer ties with relevant national ministries and commissions.

The new era implicates new requirements. A group of young African researchers constitute the fourth generation. These scholars have received strict academic training, having good foreign language communication skills with field work experience. At the same time, they are closely connected with the international academic network and highly sensitive to new research trends. Wang Haili of Beijing Normal University and Guo Dantong of Shanghai University have studied the history of ancient Egypt for a long time and published many monographs, in addition to communications within the international academia. Young scholars of the Institute of West Asia and Africa of CASS, such as Zhu Weidong, specializing in African Law, Yang Baorong, committed to African economy and China Africa relations, Wang Jinyan, exploring the tribal issues in Libya, XuGuoqing, evaluating India's African Policy, ZhiYuchen, studying the role of China's central enterprises in China-Africa relations and the basic elements in African economic development, Zhao Yating, focusing on the EU's assistance to Africa have achieved fruitful results in last three years. Others also have their own research focus.[1]

Young scholars either study on a particular country or a certain topic, such as Liu Weicai, interested in the history of Southern Africa, African integration

1 Refer to http://iwaas.cssn.cn/yjtd/zzsld/ and http://cai.cssn.cn/yjcg/xslw/.

and China-Africa relations, with a few publications, Guan Peifeng's analysis of African border disputes and settlement model, Niu Changshong's study on Zimbabwe's Higher Education, Shen Xipeng's probe on China's assistance in the construction of Tanzania-Zambia Railway, Zhou Yuyuan's assessment of African autonomy, Song Wei's analysis of the U.S. policy towards Sub-Saharan Africa after the Cold War, Cheng Cheng's focus on China-Africa Financial Cooperation, Li Pengtao's analysis of issues related to colonialism and social evolution in British Africa, Wang Congyue's interpretation of the security policies of US and EU in North Africa. The youngsters are either proficient in academic research or extensive in scope. Some of them focus on a certain country, such as Li Wengang (Nigeria), Jiang Hengkun (Sudan), Xiao Yuhua (Ethiopia), ShenXiaolei (Zimbabwe), etc. Some are interested in a specific theme, such as Li Weijian's research on Islam in Africa, Zhang Yonghong's interest in local knowledge, He Jian's study on African ocean issues, Jiang Huajie's focus on China's assistance to Africa, Liang Yijian's probe on Peer Review System, Wang Tao's interest in anti-terrorism and Zhang Jin's exploration on water environment in Africa. Zhang Yong is the first scholar to study African film and, with African scholar Dr. Hodan, has made a film well known in China and Africa. In recent years, young scholars have obtained research projects either from the National Fund or Ministry of Education. In 2019, for example, Zhou Yuyuan, Huang Yupei, Jiang Hui, Li Beilei, Zheng Xiaoxia and others won National Social Science Fund projects on African countries' relations, debt issues, African literature, Afro-American literature, African women's studies, etc.

In recent years, young scholars who studied abroad came back and have demonstrated their full strength. For example, Ha Wei, a Ph.D. in public policy from Harvard University, returned to work at the Graduate School of Education in Peking University after working in the World Bank and United Nations agencies. Tang Xiaoyang once worked in foreign research institutions and universities after receiving his Ph.D. from the New School for Social Research in New York and now works in the Department of International Relations at Tsinghua

University. After graduating from Georgetown University, Wen Shuang, once taught at New York University (Abu Dhabi) and now is teaching history at Beijing Foreign Studies University. Qiu Yu received her Ph.D. from the University of Cambridge and currently teaches in the School of Ethnology and Sociology, of Minzu University of China. Yuan Ding of Shanghai Normal University received two PhDs from Yunnan University and Leuven University at the same time. Lu Lingyu of Yunnan University received his PhD in Political Science from the University of Missouri. After graduating from Westminster University, Dr. Xiang Yu teaches in the School of Journalism and Communication of Shanghai University. Dr. Zhou Yang of Nanjing Agricultural University graduated from the University of Cologne, Germany. Chen Liang of the School of Sociology and Anthropology of Sun Yat-senUniversity, received his Ph.D. from the Australian National University, specializing in urbanization and African studies. Yang Beibei of the School of Health Care Management of Shandong University obtained her PhD of medical anthropology from Southern Methodist University. Tsinghua University's Development Program has sent out many students abroad and Dr. Gao Liangmin from the Department of Sociology is among the first to complete the degree. Liu Shaonan of the School of History, Beijing Normal University, received his PhD from Michigan State University, the best in African studies in the United States. Lian Chaoqun and Cheng Ying both obtained MA degrees from Peking University, completed their doctoral studies at University of Cambridge and University of London respectively. With his PhD in law from Peking University, Xu Liang obtained his PhD in history from Harvard University. At present, the three have become the backbone of the Center for African Studies of Peking University. Some scholars hold graduate degrees directly in Africa. For example, Dr. Sun Xiaomeng of Beijing Foreign Studies University received her MA in Hausa language in Nigeria. Zhang Qiaowen of China Africa International Business School of Zhejiang Normal University, received her Ph.D. in business management from Stellenbosch University in South Africa. Dr. Ma Xiujie of the

School of Asian and African Studies[1], Beijing Foreign Studies University studied at Rhodes University for seven years. She is proficient in English, Xhosa and Zulu, and can communicate in Ndebele and Swazi. Ma Jie of the China Institute of International Studies received her MA degree from Addis Ababa University. In addition, many students are currently studying for degrees abroad.

What's more, Chinese scholars are getting increasingly more confident in international academia.

Chinese Engagement in International Academic Community

There is no doubt that China's African study is not as advanced as expected, yet the situation is changing. Chinese scholars have actively participated in academic communications around the world and gradually gained recognition from the international academia. In addition to the participation of many Chinese scholars in international seminars, cooperation projects and African research institutions in China frequently organized academic seminars with international academic circles, especially African scholars, their engagement is reflected in three aspects: demonstrating their own characteristics in some research fields, getting more attention in the international community and increasing international publications.

Chinese scholars began to show their own characteristics, which made them outstanding in some international research fields. Justin Yifu Lin and Celestin Monga, a Cameroonian scholar, edited *The Oxford Handbook of Africa and Economics*. Works on China-Africa cooperation.were jointly edited by China and international especially African scholars. Some scholars have been invited to write relevant chapters in different encyclopedias or handbooks of various disciplines published by internationally renowned publishers, such as GeJi, Li Anshan, Xu Liang, Zhang Chun, Sun Xiaomeng, Tang Xiaoyang, Cheng Ying. They have put forward their viewpoints on different subjects such as China's African studies,

1 Was divided into School of Asian Studies and School of African studies in 2019.

China's African policy and Chinese immigration in Africa, contemporary China-Africa relations, re-conceptualizing China-Africa engagement, China's African language research, Africa's China economic and trade cooperation zone, Africa-China drama exchange. Some become editorial board members or peer reviewers of international journals. Developed governments' agencies of the U.S., U.K., France, Germany, Japan have held seminars on China-Africa relations and invited Chinese scholars or frequently sent personnel to visit China's African research institutions. The Foreign Ministries of other governments also invited Chinese scholars to explain the current situation of China-Africa cooperation.[1] All indicate the grouth of influence and competitiveness of Chinese scholars in the world.

The international academic community is paying more attention to scholars of African studies in China. Professor Na Zhong, Honorary President of the Chinese Society of African Historical Studies, was awarded the first International Prize of the Arabic Language Sharjah by UNESCO in Paris on October 25, 2001. In 2002, Yan Haiying was invited to attend the research database project of ancient Greek Olympic Games hosted by Willy Clarisse, academician of the Royal Academy of Sciences of Belgium and professor of Department of Classics of the KU Leuven. In 1998, Jin Shoufu, a Ph.D. student in Egyptology of Heidelberg University, participated in the excavation of the Tomb of Thebes Amenhotep III by the archaeology team of Waseda University in Japan. In 2000, he also participated in the excavation of the official Tomb of Luxor in Egypt by Heidelberg University. On May 24, 2013, Yang Lihua and Li Anshan, at the invitation of the African

1 For example, on June 13, 2014, Li Anshan and two Norwegian scholars in Ch. Michelsen Institute were invited to meet with officials of the Africa Department at the Norwegian Ministry of Foreign Affairs to exchange the idea of China Africa relations. On November 10, 2016, after meeting with Ms. U. Dwarka-Canabady of the Ministry of foreign Affairs of Mauritius, Li Anshan gave a lecture on "Development cooperation between China and Africa: Concept and Practice" in the Ministry of foreign affairs of Mauritius, and exchanged ideas with more than 50 diplomats including the Permanent Secretary of the Ministry of Foreign Affairs. "Professor Li Anshan, an expert on African issues, comes to Mauritius for academic exchanges", http://www.xifeizaixian.com/rzfz/2416.html.

Diplomatic Corps in China, gave keynote speech at the seminar "Pan-Africanism and African Renaissance" held at Kempinski Hotel to celebrate the Golden Jubilee of the OAU/AU on September 9, 2013.[1] Zhu Weidong was appointed to the International Commercial Panel by the Arbitration Foundation of Southern Africa (AFSA).[2] On September 19, 2013, Li Anshan was invited to participate in the "symposium to celebrate the 15th anniversary of the establishment of diplomatic relations between China and South Africa" and delivered a speech at the new book launch edited by South African scholar F.Y. Yazini and him in the building of the Ministry of Foreign Affairs of South Africa.[3] On November 3, 2013, Li Anshan was invited by the Director General of UNESCO, Ms. Irina Bokova, to participate in the International Scientific Committee of UNESCO General History of Africa (volume 9, later expanded to 9-11 volumes), and was elected Vice Chairman of the Committee at the first meeting held in Brazil.[4] The McMillan Center of Yale University invited Li Anshan and Ibrahim Gambari, former Foreign Minister of Nigeria and former Under Secretary General of the United Nations to co-chair the international seminar on "Africa China Relations: Balance, Growth and Sustainable Future" held in Nigeria during March 15-18, 2016, and the seminar

1 "African Diplomatic Mission in China held the Golden Jubilee of the OAU/AU Seminar in Beijing", http://www.chinafrica.cn/chinese/zxxx/txt/2013-05/27/content_544893.htm.

2 "Zhu Weidong of Center for African Law was appointed to the International Commercial Panel by the Arbitration Foundation of Southern Africa", Xiangtan University Law School, November 4, 2013. http://law.xtu.edu.cn/infoshow-17-3869-0.html.

3 "China-South African held seminar to celebrate the 15th anniversary of establishment of diplomatic relations", Chinanet, September 20, 2013; http://finance.china.com.cn/roll/20130920/1825806.shtml; https://caspu.pku.edu.cn/cn/zxlt/dwjl/230178.html.

4 "Report of the meeting:International Scientific Committee for the drafting of Volume IX of the General History of Africa", Salvador, 20-24 November 2013; ChenZhenyun, "Let the great African history tell the future——Interview with Li Anshan, Vice Chairman of the International Scientific Committee of UNESCO General History of Africa (9-11 Vols.)", *Peking University Gazette*, January 10, 2020. See also the net version in The Paper website, https://m.thepaper.cn/newsDetail_forward_6290328?from=singlemessage.

held at Beijing Forum of Peking University in November 2017.[1] In 2018, Liu Haifang was appointed member of the Executive Board of the CA/AC Research Network. It is encouraging that some young scholars' capabilities have been recognized by the international academia. For example, Cheng Ying's doctoral thesis won the Best Doctoral Thesis Award of the Lagos Studies Association, the first among Chinese scholars. Dr. Liu Shaonan was the first Asian scholar to receive the Graduate Student Paper Prize Winner at the 2018 annual meeting of the U.S. African Studies Association.[2] Surprisingly Chinese PhD student Xiao Gang won the same prize in the following year. Dr. Zhou Yang's thesis on cross-cultural marriage between China and Africa was awarded the "sehr gut: 1.0 (excellent)" level.

The number international publication of Chinese scholars is also growing. In the 1990s, Chinese scholars published few articles in international academia. In 1995, Yan Haiying of Peking University presented a paper at the 7th International Egyptologist Conference held in Cambridge, which attracted the attention of the international academic community. After graduating from the University of Toronto and working at Peking University in 1994, Li Anshan put forward his own views on Ghana's history in his new book published both in Chinese and English. Since the beginning of 21st century, the research on Africa or China-Africa relations has been strengthened, and scholars have published more and more works in international academia, presenting their opinions in the forms of monographs, anthologies or papers. For example, Jin Shoufu of Fudan University studies ancient Egyptian papyrus documents and theocracy. Li Anshan's monographs probe the colonial rule, rural protest in Ghana , his books on history

1 "Professor Li Anshan, Chair of the Chinese Society of African Historical Studies, was invited to co-chair the seminar on China-African Relations", World History Research of China Net, http://iwh.cssn.cn/yjdt/yjdt_xstt_gx_dfsk/201604/t20160413_2964555.shtml. In 2014, Li Anshan gave lectures/speeches as AFRASO Professor at Frankfurt University. In 2015, during former UN Secretary General Kofi Annan's visit, Peking University sent him Li Anshan's monographs on Ghanaian history both in Chinese and English as a gift.

2 "Graduate Student Paper Prize Winners", https://africanstudies.org/awards-prizes/graduate-student-paper-prize/graduate-student-paper-prize-winners/. Accessed 2019-6-26.

of Chinese in Africa and China-Africa relations are both published in Engish in U.S. and South Africa, Yan Haiying states her own view on Ptolemy's steles. They have also introduced the research status of China to international circle, such as Yan Haiying's research on ancient Egyptian cultural relics collected in China, Wang Haili's analysis on Chinese research methods of Egyptian hieroglyphs and the introduction of Professor Liu Wenpeng, Wen Shuang's introduction to Chinese Arabic research, Li Anshan's review of African studies in China in different periods.

The international academia is paying more attention to increasing Chinese works. Their papers mainly focus on China-Africa relations. K.K. Prah, a Ghanaian scholar now working in South Africa, Kenyan scholar J. Shikwati, German Heinrich-Böll Foundation and African NGO Faham made special collections for seminars on China-Africa Cooperation which reflects the understanding of China-Africa cooperation between the two sides. Three collections of papers jointly compiled by Chinese scholars with South African and Ethiopian scholars express the representative opinions of both sides on China Africa cooperation. These anthologies include the papers of Zeng Qiang, Yang Lihua, An Chunying, He Wenping, Hong Yonghong, Li Baoping, Li Zhibiao, Zhang Yongpeng, Liu Hongwu, Shi Lin, Zhang Chun, Liang Yijian, Tang Xiaoyang, Xiao Yuhua, Zhi Yingbiao, LuoJianbo, Li Xinfeng, Wang Nan, Pang Zhongying, Wang Xuejun, Li Anshan, Xiao Hongyu, Xu Liang, Zeng Aiping, Zhang Weijie, etc., which show Chinese understanding of Sino-African partnership. In general, Chinese scholars discuss China's African policy, its role and influence, macro analysis of BRICs Cooperation, international cooperation or aid, industry and mining, economic technology, medical and health, culture and education, law and governance, Two-way migration.

Young scholars back to China from Abroad have published many articles internationally. Wen Shuang focuses on the history of China-Egypt relations and Asia-Africa exchanges. Zhang Qiaowen has noted the role of China-Africa Development Fund. Cheng Ying specializes in Nigerian drama and the exchange of Chinese and African Drama. Xu Liang studies the economic development of South Africa and the role of Chinese. Tang Xiaoyang's book on coevolutionary pragmatism and articles on China-Africa relations are noticed among scholars. Lian Chaoqun's articles are on Arab politics and culture in English and Arabic. Qiu Yu discusses social aspects of China-Africa contact, especially corporate ethics (2018). Yuan Ding made an English proper noun "Guoke" (过客) on the basis of his own study[1] and others' previous research especially Niu Dong's study on Africans in Guangzhou which took the Chinese concept " 过客 " with English equivalent "transient" in his English article. Liu Shaonan examined the contribution of overseas Chinese to Nigerian local society. *Journal of Ancient Civilizations*, a journal in English issued by the Institute for the History of Ancient Civilizations in Northeast Normal University, published relevant articles. *World History Studies*, an English journal of the Institute of World History, CASS, also published articles on Africa. Other English journals in China such as *Contemporary International Relations* by China Institutes of Contemporary International Relations, *China International Studies* by China Institute of international Studies, *Global Review* by Shanghai Institutes of International Studies and *China International Strategy Review* by Institute of International and Strategical Studies of Peking University, publish related articles occasionally. *Journal of China-Africa Studies* (in Chinese, English & French), newly published by China-Africa Institute, will provide a new platform for the international exchange of China's African studies.

African Research Institutions in China

There are three pioneers in African research institutions, the West Asia Africa Research Group of the Chinese Academy of Sciences set up in 1956 and the Institute of West Asia and African Studies established in 1961; the African History

1 "Yuan Ding: A 'GuoKe's self-description", January 18, 2018. https://www.sohu.com/a/217568807_329964.

Research Office of Peking University set up in 1958 and the Institute of Afro-Asian Studies established in 1965; the African Geography Research Office of Nanjing University set up in 1964 and the Institute of African Studies established in 1992. After the Reform and Opening up, many universities have established teaching and research institutions related to Africa, including Xiangtan University (1978), East China Normal University (1985), Shanghai Normal University (1998), Yunnan University (1998), etc. With the establishment of the FOCAC and the rapid development of China-Africa relations, African research institutions have sprung up, such as Center for African Studies of Peking University (2000), Center for African Education Studies of Zhejiang Normal University (2003), renamed as the Institute of African Studies in 2007, Center for African Vocational Education Studies of Tianjin University of Technology and Education (2005), renamed as Center of African Union Studies in 2012, Center for African Agricultural Studies of Nanjing Agricultural University (2006), Center for African Studies of Yunnan University (2007), Center for African Studies of East China Normal University (2010), renamed as Institute of African Studies in 2011, etc. African language teaching started early in China, mainly Swahili and Hausa. Beijing Foreign Studies University, Tianjin Foreign Studies University, Communication University of China, Peking University, Shanghai International Studies University, etc., now begin to attach more importance to African languages. Some students are sent to Africa to learn Swahili, Amharic, Hausa, Yoruba, Zulu, Xhosa and other African languages. In addition to government ministries and subordinate institutions (such as the Development Research Center of the State Council and the Party School of Central Committee of CP), more than 30 African research institutions have been established, with journals, weekly reports, annual reports, websites and various publications.

Among the African research institutions, the Institute of West Asia and Africa of CASS has an irreplaceable position. In addition to its outstanding institutions, personnel, conditions and funding projects, it has published *Annual Report on Development in the Middle East and Africa* or *Yellow Book of Middle East and Africa* since 1998, covering the current situations and characteristics of

African affairs every year. In 2012, *Yellow book of Africa* or *Annual Report on Development of Africa* was separated thus became an important reference for African studies and the forecast of African affairs. In recent years, its journal *West Asia and Africa* (1980 -) has gained great influence under the editorship of An Chunying and Zhan Shiming, greatly promoted the study of African issues and China-Africa relations. In 2019, 10 articles of the journal were reprinted by *Chinese Social Science Abstracts* and *Periodical Materials Photocopied by Renmin University of China*. The China-Africa Institute, founded on the basis of the IWAAS in 2019, has made its African research more focused and interacted frequently with African academic institutions. The Institute has launched two batches of cooperative research projects with African scholars (4 in the first batch and 14 in the second), covering political, economic, social, cultural and other aspects. The newly founded flagship *Journal of China-Africa Studies*" will adhere to "the principles of academic quality, innovation and openness, the journal will publish high-quality academic papers on Africa studies, China studies, and China-Africa relations by scholars from all over the world", "dedicated to promoting outstanding academic works, facilitating academic exchanges, reflecting new academic trends", which is believed to provide a platform for China-Africa cooperation.[1]

Center for African Studies of Peking University was established in 2000. Prior to the establishment of the FOCAC, it was arranged to hold "International Forum on China Africa Cooperation", and has carried out long-term academic cooperation with key African countries such as Egypt, South Africa and Nigeria. In addition to *Annual Review of African Studies in China*, PKU African Tele-Info as a weekly has been operational for nearly 10 years and published more than 400 issues in electronic form with more than 6000 users, which has a great impact

1 The institutions involved in the first and second batches of joint-research projects are those of South Africa, Egypt, Ethiopia, Kenya, Tanzania, Zambia, Cameroon, Mauritius, Morocco, etc. China-Africa Institute issued the notice of the third batch of joint-research projects in December 2019. http://cai.cssn.cn/lhyj/jr1/.

at home and abroad. The Institute of African Studies of Nanjing University has conducted fruitful works on African economic geography. It began to publish an annual report *African Development Studies* in 2017, and also published the compilation of research materials on African economic geography and regional development in 2019 (6 volumes) including the papers and reports on African issue not published in the public during 1964-1986, which has important academic value and practical significance. In Xiangtan University, after the establishment of the Center for African Legal and Social Studies on the basis of its African studies, the Center has published *African Law Review*, focusing on legal research in Africa, with rich achievements. Center for African Studies of Shanghai Normal University has achieved great progress in recent years. In addition to holding regular African Economic seminars, it has also published *African Economic Review* (2012-) and *African Economic Development Report* (2014-). The African Institute of East China Normal University has its focus on East Africa, mainly in Tanzania, Uganda and other countries. The research team has translated four volumes of Julius Nyerere's works and held seminars on African art. As a new force, the Institute of African Studies of Zhejiang Normal University has made great achievements. It publishes *African Studies* and *Annual Report on the Development of Africa* and "African Studies Series", established African Museum and many research centers on education, film, anthropology, etc. Center for African Studies of Yunnan University has produced many works. In recent years, it has absorbed talents and began to explore its own focus according to its geographical characteristics and conditions research team. School of Asian and African Studies of Beijing Foreign Studies University (now the independent School of African Studies) has long had the characteristics of African language teaching and scientific research. It publishes *Asian and African Studies* (2007-), sent teachers and students to study local languages in Africa. Center for African Media Studies of Communication University of China was founded in 2012, which has trained a lot of professionals for China-Africa news communication and exchange.

Newly established African research institutions put emphasis on strengthening their own characteristics, some of them make full use of the advantages of setting up Confucius Institutes in African countries. Center of African Union Studies of Tianjin University of Technology and Education makes full use of the Confucius Institute in Ethiopia. On the one hand, it promotes the development of African educational cooperation. On the other hand, it is committed to carrying out research on African Union Organizations in politics, economy, culture and other aspects to provide intellectual support for national strategy. Yangzhou University established Center for Sudanese Studies in 2012 and recruited two Sudanese researchers to cooperate with Sudanese universities. Its researches cover the history of Sudan in the colonial period, Islamic movement, foreign relations, higher education, the dilemma after the political mutation, the annual report, the manual of the religious situation, etc. Center of Research for Madagascar of Jiangxi Normal University employs two Malagasy researchers to conduct a follow-up study on Madagascar based on the ten-year experience and achievements of Confucius Institute in Madagascar. Its website has its own characteristics, especially the introduction of relevant laws and regulations of Madagascar. The School of Sociology and Anthropology of Sun Yat-sen University, taking full use of its own advantages, has held two successive seminars on "Ancient and Modern China-Africa Relations" focusing on "field research methodology of African anthropology". It has also conducted anthropological field research in Ethiopia and archaeological excavation with international scholars in Kenya.[1] Founded in 2016, the Institute for African Studies of Guangdong University of Foreign Studies pays great attention to social practice and has carried out a variety of activities at home and abroad in recent years. Center for African Studies of Jinan University and Center for African Studies of Wuhan University mainly rely on foreign language research and teaching capabilities, the study focusing on African French speaking countries. Center for African Coastal States Studies of Zhejiang

1 Wang Xiaopeng& Lu Duobao, "Remains of Chinese consanguinity during the Zheng He's period are discovered in Kenya", July 29, 2017. http://www.xinhuanet.com/world/2017-07/29/c_1121400232.htm.

Ocean University focuses on nine coastal States, including Senegal. Research institutions of China Foreign Affairs University, Hunan Normal University and others are also following up.[1]

African study in the School of Social and Anthropology of Xiamen University has been fruitful due to the invitation of Professor Augustin Holl (with a Chinese name Gao Chang) to join the team. Professor Gao Chang is a Cameroonian scholar and a famous archaeologist. He once served as Professor/Curator of the Museum of Anthropology of the University of Michigan (2000-2008) and Vice President of Université Paris X (2012-2014). At the invitation of Xiamen University, he resigned from CNRS (Centre National de la Recherche Scientifique) in 2017 and went to the Department of Anthropology and Ethnology of Xiamen University for teaching. Later, he donated his archaeological and cultural collections to Xiamen University for teaching and research and established an archaeological anthropology laboratory. He led Chinese students to Senegal for archaeological excavation in the summer of 2018 and published a large number of papers and research reports in international academic journals.[2] In 2017, the University of Electronic Science and Technology of China established Center for West African Studies (CWAS) together with five universities in Ghana, e.g., University of Ghana (UG), University of Cape Coast (UCC), Ghana Institute of Management and Public Administration (GIMPA), University of Education at Winneba (UEW), University for Development Studies (UDS), The two sides jointly held a seminar to promote the cooperation in education and scientific research. At present, CWAS regularly issues annual reports in Chinese and English. One of CWAS' innovative ways is to make African and Chinese scholars publish articles together. This joint research has turned out to be with good results.

1 For details, please refer to "Notes on the chronicle of African studies in China since 1949: Taking the research institutions and academic journals as the main line", https://book.douban.com/review/10367544/.

2 "Featured Interview: Professor Augustin F. C. Holl", Office of International Cooperation and Exchange/Office of Taiwan, Hong Kong and Macao Affairs, November 1, 2019, https://ice.xmu.edu.cn/en/info/1015/1146.htm.

New trends of African research in China

The most important factor in the study of liberal arts and social sciences is its relevance to human society. In terms of studies on regions and countries, subsistence development and environment (including nature, society and international community) are important concerns. I have studies the current situation and new interests of China's African Studies, such as China-Africa relations, country studies, African history, political economy, international relations and legal Studies. This part will briefly introduce the new trends of research fields and topics.

The study of Africa in China began with the study of Egyptian history. Egyptology rose with the slave trade and European colonial expansion. The colonial rule made Egypt separate from Africa and extend to Europe. With the efforts of African scholars including Egyptian scholars, UNESCO General History of Africa (Volumes 1-8) have brought Egypt back to Africa from the perspective of academic history. Starting from Xia Nai, the "father of Egyptology in China", with the development of Na Zhong, Liu Wenpeng, Yang Haocheng and other scholars of older generation, it has been carried forward under the inheritance of Yan Haiying, Jin Shoufu, Bi Jiankang and others. Lin Zhichun, Professor of Northeast Normal University, has made outstanding contributions to Egyptology in China, and trained such backbones as LingfuRuoming, Yan Haiying, Jin Shoufu, Li Dongxiao, Li Mo, etc..[1] A new generation of scholars and their researches are emerging, such as Guo Dandong's concerns on economic history, Wang Haili's emphasis on social history, and GuoZilin's interest on autocratic monarchy. On modern and contemporary history of Egypt, Bi Jiankang analyzed the political

1 The Institute for the History of Ancient Civilizations of Northeast Normal University has set up a special experimental class for young scholars, who gradually grow to be the backbone of the study of ancient world history in China. It also runs an English journal, *Journal of Ancient Civilizations* (JAC)to provide a platform for the study of Egyptology, Assyriology and Hittist studies, etc., which has greatly promoted the study of Egyptology in China.

stability of Egyptian society, Wang Tai paid attention to the interaction among the three basic forces on the Egyptian political stage: state, society and political Islam. The research team in Egyptian study is relatively neat, and the subjects are diversified.[1]

Anthropological/ethnological and sociological research on Africa is becoming increasingly active. Shi Lin and Zhuang Chenyan of Minzu University of China have probed ethnological methodology and African ethnic/national issues. Li Zhigang and Niu Dong have analyzed Africans's existence in China. Xu Wei has probed African anthropology, ethnicity issue and ethnic relations, especially that in Botswana through field work.[2] More importantly, in recent years, a number of anthropology/ethnology doctors have returned to China, such as Qiu Yu, Yuan Ding, Chen Liang, Yang Beibei, Zhou Yang, etc. These young scholars discussed the social interaction of two-way immigrants, the survival track of Africans in Guangzhou, African ethnography and urbanization, the health challenges and medical strategies of new Chinese immigrants in Africa, and the two-way cultural adaptation of Chinese/African families. Dr. Lei Wen transferred from development studies to anthropology research.[3] From 2015 to 2018, Gao Liangmin of Tsinghua University conducted ethnographic research in Tanzania, Kenya and surrounding areas. These scholars have brought new horizon to the study of Africa and China-Africa relations. Topics such as ethnography, ethnic relations, environmental adaptation, conflict mediation have been brought into the research field. Zhejiang Normal University established the Center for African Anthropology Studies and held various academic activities. Minzu University of China, Sun Yat-sen University and Xiamen University held lectures, forums and seminars on African anthropology/ethnology/Sociology. Cross-border ethnic flow, conflict, adaptation

---

1 For Egyptology in China, refer to "Entry into Egyptology in China", http://www.cssn.cn/zt/zt_xkzt/zt_lsxzt/zjzgajx/zgajxxz/.

2 "XuWei: I and African anthropology——Era, subject, platform and individual", https://new.qq.com/omn/20180125/20180125B02BUI.html.

3 "Lei Wen: My anthropological time", January 15, 2018. http://www.sohu.com/a/216859357_501399.

and mediation, interaction between nomads and settlers, complementarity between urban and rural areas, the local wisdom to solve the contradictions between human and nature and among human themselves, and the role of African immigrant groups, should be gradually included in research scope.

One of the main characteristics of China's African studies is its close connection with African reality. The interaction between politics and economy has always been the research focus, including various topics such as African leaders and political governance, party politics and development strategies, democracy and corruption, NGO, power inheritance and political stability, national issues and national construction, non-traditional security and counter-terrorism, etc. With the signing of the African Continental Free Trade Agreement, the topic of African integration is becoming increasingly important, which is reflected in the relations between AU and UN and other international organizations, AU and the International Criminal Court, AU and its member states, AU and African regional organizations. African law research is one of the important areas in recent years. With the strengthening of China-Africa relation, more and more Chinese enterprises and immigrants are entering Africa, hoping to understand the laws of African countries, thus arousing scholars' attention to this issue. The "African Law" series edited by Hong Yonghong provides a platform for the dissemination of African legal knowledge and discussion. Scholars such as Zhu Weidong, Xia Xinhua, Li Bojun, have not only translated African laws or materials of legal systems, but also published many articles on international arbitration and dispute settlement. Chinese scholars should gradually strengthen their researches on legal settcements of international disputes, such as the issue of Chagos Islands.

The study of African economy involves such respects as industry, agriculture, marine fishery, water environment, small enterprises, poverty reduction, technology transfer, food security, population dividend, debt sustainability, international cooperation and assistance, etc. Lin Yifu's new structural economics shows Chinese scholars' view on world economy, especially African economy from a unique perspective. Li Xiaoyun's team made efforts to explore the issue of aid effectiveness through the practice of increasing food production in Tanzania. We should strengthen our research on African Continental Free Trade Agreement and its effect. The free trade zone will cover a market with a population of 1.2 billion and a GDP of 2.5 trillion US dollars. The Secretariat of the free trade zone is located in Ghana, and its spillover effect cannot be ignored. The Economic Community of West African States (ECOWAS) is a regional organization with rather quick integration, its 2019 Ministerial Conference reaffirmed that it would speed up the process of monetary integration and launch a single currency in 2020. Its role and trend need to be explored. The study of countries and regions (such as the horn of Africa, the Mediterranean coast, the Great Lakes region, the Sahel region, the Congo River Basin, the Gulf of Guinea, the West Indian Ocean Islands) is of great importance. With a general understanding of the continent, we should put emphasis on its characteristics, such as the relationship between African Franc countries and France, the economic diversification of resource countries such as Nigeria and Angola, the marine resource development of coastal countries, the intermediary role of Mauritius (development model, capital, goods, finance, etc.), biodiversity and social development of Madagascar, governance model of Rwanda, immigration economy of South Africa, the role of African diaspora especially those in U.S. and Europe, etc.

African literature is a new field. Except the introduction of a few works at the end of the 19th century and the few published in *The Eastern Miscellany* in the early 20th century, the study of African literature in China began in 1960s and the systematic research after 1980s. From 1986 to 2016, important African writers were explored and about 990 papers on African literature covering 16 African countries were published in Chinese journals. The translation and introduction of African works focus on the works of protest against colonialism or national independence, African tradition or local culture and Nobel Prize winners, with the characteristics of more English works than French works, more male works than female works, more novels than dramas, etc., and there are various projects to study Africa including African Americans. For example, 445 articles were published about Nobel Prize Winner Coetzee from January 1986 to June 2016 and research works are also concentrated on Coetzee. Very few take notice of African black writers. The two works edited by Zhu Zhenwu reflect the general situation of China's research on African English Literature. In recent years, African literature study has expanded from Nobel laureates to popular writers, from literature research to critical theory, from general study to specfic study. Scholars such as Yao Feng, Sun Xiaomeng, Wang Lin translated *African Literature - An Anthology of Criticism and theory* edited by Tejumola Olaniyan and Ato Quayson, the first collection to comprehensively introduce African literary theory and criticism, emphasizing the uniqueness of African philology and highlighting the local characteristics of Africa.

There has been a discussion about the possibility of Africa taking full play of its advantages to develop. If the answer is yes, what are the advantages? How to use these advantages? Political science should be deeply explored in the aspects of the balance of African political tradition and its rationality, the advantages and disadvantages of the contemporary introduction of Western democratic elections, the enthusiasm of people to participate in politics and the operation of different power groups. African countries have encountered various problems, but they have been resisting external interference and hoping to overcome the difficulties with their own efforts. This growing sense of self-consciousness, with Ethiopia and Rwanda as models, reflects Africa's exploration of a development path that suits its own conditions. African localization and autonomy is another important issue, including African perspective in international development cooperation. Why can all forms African culture survive in the economical backwardness and spread and flourish all over the world? Cultural studies should not only recognize the diversity and particularity of African cultures, but also evaluate its appeal, adaptability, penetration and influence, including the boundaries of African philosophy, religion and tradition. International politics and international relations should strengthen the discussion of Africa's role in international arena, including the role of Africa at the United Nations and the balanced relationship between Africa and major powers. The Franc area in Africa is extremely dependent on

France in all aspects, which is a dependence imposed by the former suzerain. All these should be explored with attention.

Conclusion

China's African studies have gained new momentum. It must be acknowledged that African studies are still rather weak in China, the study of China-Africa relations tends to be too general and lacks depth. Policy oriented research have to be objective and based on profound academic research. More attention should be paid to countries or topics, as well as solid field work and interdisciplinary research. China's African studies should deal with the following relations: academic discussion and social practice, knowledge popularization and in-depth research, case study and theoretical generalization, micro analysis and macro generalization, country, region and global research, etc. We look forward to comprehensive academic cooperation with African counterparts and international academicions. I am full of confidence for African Studies in China. [1]

Resume of the Author

Li Anshan, professor of the School of International Studies, Peking University. He has published works on African history and historiography, African nationalism, and Chinese overseas and world history in Chinese and English. He is President of Chinese Society of African Historical Studies, Vice President of the International Scientific Committee of UNESCO General History of Africa (Vol.IX-XI), Vice President of China Society for Asia-Africa, Vice President of China Society for African Studies, Vice President of the Overseas Chinese History Society of China, etc.

1 Zhang Mengying& Wu He, "China's African studies and my research path——Interview with Peking University Professor and Director of Center for African Studies Li Anshan", Chinese Social Sciences Net, November 9, 2017. http://www.cssn.cn/gj/gj_hqxx/201711/t20171109_3737563.shtml.

National Societies on African Studies in China

Chinese Society of Asian and African Studies

I. Introduction

The Chinese Society of Asian and African Studies (CSAAS) is one of the earliest academic groups established in China to study international issues. Under the affectionate care of Premier Zhou Enlai and Vice Premier Chen Yi and the proposition and support of multiple famous scholars in domestic academic and cultural circles, the CSAAS was established in Beijing on April 19, 1962, with Zhou Yang as the director of the first council. Its establishment marked the arrival of a comprehensive, systematic and organized stage of China's research on Asian and African countries. When it was founded, the society had more than 500 members, covering more than 20 provinces (autonomous regions) and municipalities across the country. During the "Cultural Revolution"(1966-1976), the society ceased all its activities, and in December 1984, it went back into operation. In March 1986, the CSAAS held its second corference of representatives in Beijing, which revised and adopted the new constitution of the society, and made propositions for the society's future activities. With these measures, the society resumed its normal and planned work. On August 1, 1991, the CSAAS was re-examined and approved by the Ministry of Civil Affairs as a legitimate national academic social organization. In September 1999, in accordance with the *Regulations on the Registration and Management of Social Organizations* of the Ministry of Civil Affairs and the revised *Administrative Rules of the Chinese Academy of Social Sciences on Social Organizations*, and on the basis of discussion in its standing council, the CSAAS revised its constitution. Upon the approval of the Chinese Academy of Social Sciences and the Ministry of Civil Affairs, the CSAAS was successfully registered again on January 20, 2000. Since the establishment of the society, a total of seven representative meetings have been held. On July 13, 2018, the "Seventh Representative Meeting of the CSAAS and Symposium on Asian-African Situations" was held in Beijing. 107 experts and scholars were elected as members of the seventh council of the society. Zhang Hongming was elected as the president of the council; Liu Zhongmin, Liu Hongwu, Xiao Xian, Mu Tao, Zhang Zhongxiang, Zhang Zhenke, Li Anshan, Li Xinfeng, Yang Guang, Hong Yonghong, Xu Weizhong, Guo Zhizheng, and Huang Minxing were elected as vice presidents; and Zhan Shiming was elected as the secretary-general.

The CSAAS aims to promote Chinese research on political, economic, cultural, religious and social conditions of Asia and Africa as well as the countries in the region, and actively carries out academic exchanges with people from home and abroad. For the past decades, the CSAAS has mainly carried out work in the following five areas: (1) establishing the *CSAAS Newsletter* to introduce its members' activities and researches, publish academic achievements of domestic and foreign scholars, exchange latest information on Asian-African research, and report on the work and research of the CSAAS, with a total of 15 issues compiled and distributed till now; (2) holding academic seminars; (3) holding academic lectures; (4) carrying out international academic exchanges; and (5) compiling and printing collections of academic papers.

In recent years, the academic activities held by the CSAAS have become more frequent and abundant. It has successively hosted (or co-hosted) the Seminar on "Asian-African Cooperation in the New International Environment" (November 2012), the Seminar on "Fifty Years Development of the Organization of African

Unity/the African Union and Asia-Africa Cooperation" (May 2013), the High-end Seminar on "the 'Belt and Road' Initiative and Asian-African Cooperation in the New Era" to commemorate the 60th Anniversary of the Bandung Conference (April 2015), the Academic Seminar on "Expansion and Maintenance of China's Interests in Africa in the New Era" (September 2016), the Academic Seminar on "Francophone Countries of Africa: Development and Cooperation" (August 2018), the Academic Seminar on "Studies of African Key Countries" (December 2018), the Academic Seminar on "Major Practical and Hot Issues on the African Situation", the Academic Seminar on "Seventy Years of China's African Studies: Retrospection and Outlook", and other major academic seminars. In addition, the CSAAS has invited the head of the African Department of the Ministry of Foreign Affairs to give lectures on "African Situation and Relations with Africa" every year, which has had a considerable influence over the circle of African studies in Beijing.

II. Contact Information

Website: http://iwaas.cssn.cn/xsst/zgyfxh/

Contact Person: Zhan Shiming; Tel: +86-10-87421036/7; Email: zhansm@cass.org.cn

Correspondence Address: China-Africa Institute, Building 3, No. 1 National Stadium Road, Chaoyang District, Beijing (100101), P. R. China.

Chinese Research for African Affairs

I. Introduction

China Society for African Studies is a national organization registered with the Ministry of Civil Affairs and supervised by the Ministry of Education. It was established in 1979, at the beginning of reform and opening up, as an early national academic organization specializing in African studies. Since 1979, Professor Zhang Tongzhu of the Institute of African Studies of Nanjing University, Researcher Chen Gongyuan of the Institute of West Asian and African Studies of the Chinese Academy of Social Sciences, and former deputy director general AnYongyu of the Ministry of Foreign Affairs successively served as the president of the society. The secretariat of the society is affiliated with the Institute of African Studies of Nanjing University. The current council of the society was registered with the Ministry of Civil Affairs in March 2016. The incumbent president is Mr. Wei Jianguo, former Vice Minister of the Ministry of Commerce, and there are currently 280 members in the society.

China Society for African Studies is an academic group that studies African economic and social development issues. It is mainly composed of experts and scholars of African studies from domestic universities and colleges, research institutions, time-honored media and relevant institutions. As a national organization of African studies covering different disciplines and fields, the society aims to give full play to its advantages in the academic circle; carry out comprehensive research on African economic and social development strategies; focus on China-Africa cooperation strategies, investment and trade in Africa, and other hot issues related to African development; and carry out academic exchanges and discussions. The main business of the society includes academic exchanges, theoretical research, professional training, international cooperation, and consultancy services. The main academic activities include organizing academic seminars and lectures, providing consultancy services for relevant departments and institutions, and promoting international academic exchanges and cooperation.

Since its establishment, China Society for African Studies has held dozens of national and international academic conferences on African studies, conducting academic discussion and exchanges on African development, African economy, African modernization, China-Africa relations, Africa and globalization, and other issues. The society has organized researchers to publish *Atlas of Africa*, *Research on African Economic and Social Development Strategies*, *African Economic Development Strategy*, *Concise Encyclopedia of Sub-Saharan Africa*, and other monographs and reference books. Since 2017, the society has published collections of *African Development Studies* from time to time. The Institute of West Asian and African Studies of the Chinese Academy of Social Sciences is one of the founding partners and the most important member of the society. It has established two academic journals, namely, *West Asia and Africa*, and *Journal of China-Africa Studies*; and is a domestic key academic platform for African studies. Nanjing University, with which the secretariat of the society is affiliated, has published *African Petroleum Geography*, *African Agricultural Geography*, *African Physical Geography*, *Atlas of Africa*, *Research on African Resource Development and China-Africa Energy Cooperation Security* (series), *African Agriculture Pictorial*, *Compilation of Research Results on African Economic Geography and Regional Development* (6-volume edition), *Three Countries in Central Africa: Leaping from Tribes to Modern Life*, *Essay Compilation Series of Exploring Africa and Seeking Development Forum*, and other books on the basis of its Center of African Studies and related areas of studies (economic geography, world history, international relations, and international trade). Since the establishment of the society, with the support of the organization with which it is affiliated and relevant national departments, all staff and member units have worked hard to forge ahead, making important contributions to the development of China's African studies.

II. Contact Information

Website: http://www.chinasas.org.cn

Contact Person: Zhang Zhenke; Tel: +86-25-89686694; Email: casnju@126.com

Correspondence Address: Center of African Studies at Nanjing University/ China Society for African Studies, No. 163 Xianlin Road, Nanjing City, Jiangsu Province (210023), P. R. China.

Chinese Society of African Historical Studies

I. Introduction

The Chinese Society of African Historical Studies is a national non-governmental academic organization registered with the Ministry of Civil Affairs.

The society was founded in 1980 and is located at the School of International Studies, Peking University. Currently, there are 260 members. Its leading body is the council elected by all members. The current council, which is the tenth, was elected in October 2017.

The council hires top experts, Professor Lu Tingen and Professor Ning Sao, as its honorary presidents, and hires Researcher Peng Kunyuan, Professor Gu Zhangyi, Professor Zheng Jiaxin, Professor Li Guangyi, Professor Zhang Xiang, Mr. He Liehui, Professor Xu Yongzhang, Ambassador Huang Shejiao, Ambassador Xu Mengshui, Ambassador Liu Guijin, Researcher Yang Lihua, Professor Shu Yunguo, Researcher Zhang Hongming, Professor Li Zhongren and Professor Liu Hongwu as advisors.

The incumbent president is Dr. Li Anshan, an authoritative expert well-known at home and abroad and a professor at Peking University.

The society aims to, following the policy of "letting a hundred flowers blossom and a hundred schools of thought contend", coordinate and promote academic exchanges at home and abroad, enhance the depth of African studies, promote the development of China-Africa relations, and contribute to China's reform and opening up as well as socialist modernization. The main responsibilities of the society include uniting and organizing the teachers, researchers of and other relevant practioners African history across the country to carry out research on African history and other African issues; organizing and holding academic seminars and lectures on the subject; organizing its members to write, edit and translate monographs, papers, reports and other materials related to the subject; providing consultancy services for relevant departments and institutions; promoting international academic exchanges, etc.

Since its establishment 40 years ago, the society has held more than 30 national academic conferences, initiating academic discussions on the trend of socialist thoughts in Africa, national liberation movements in Africa, the class structure of Africa, political transformation and political development of Africa, African modernization and economic development issues, globalization and Africa, China-

Africa relations, the 60 years of the African Union, the relationship between Africa and the outside world, urbanization of Africa and the "Belt and Road" Initiative, and other topics. The society has compiled and published *Collection of Essays on African History* (SDX Joint Publishing Company, 1982 edition), *Africa* (three-volume edition, East China Normal University Press, 1995 edition), *Collection of Essays of the Chinese Society of African Historical Studie*s (2015), [Social Sciences Academic Press (China), 2016 edition], African studies series (East China Normal University Press) and other academic monographs with major influence; led the writing of *Annals of Africa*, *Catalogue of Chinese Literature on African Studies*, and other reference books; organized and coordinated the translation and introduction of academic masterpieces such as the eight-volume *General History of Africa* compiled by the United Nations Educational, Scientific and Cultural Organization; and published 28 issues of its society journal—*Studies of African History*. The society has actively encouraged and organized domestic scholars to travel to Africa for academic investigations and lectures, and invited well-known foreign scholars to China for academic visits and academic reports, making important contributions to scientific research, talent training and disciplinary construction on African history.

II. Contact Information

Website: http://iwh.cssn.cn/xh_zx/xh_zx_zgfzsyjh/

Contact Person: Liu Lan; Tel: +86-10-87421031; Email: liulan@cass.org.cn

Correspondence Address: Institute of World History, Chinese Academy of Social Sciences, No. 1 National Stadium Road, Chaoyang District, Beijing (100101), P. R. China.

Research Organizations on African Studies in China

Center of West Asian & North African Studies, Anhui University

I. Introduction

The Center of West Asian & North African Studies at Anhui University is a specialized interdisciplinary research institution based on the resources and strengths of international studies in the fields of international relations, economics, law, history and French in Anhui University, and was approved by Anhui University on May 13, 2015. As one of the regional research centers under the Center for Regional and Country-Specific Studies at Anhui University, it mainly studies the development and changes of West Asia and North Africa as well as individual countries there in various aspects, and focuses on the studies of the investment environment of West Asian and North African countries that are closely related to the social and economic development of Anhui Province from economic, political, legal, cultural, and social aspects, providing reference and consultancy for the local government of Anhui Province in its investment cooperation and work of foreign affairs in the region.

The center currently has four full-time researchers and four part-time researchers. In the research team, there are not only young academic backbones with solid professional foundation and great prospects but also experienced and vigorous academic and disciplinary leaders. They are pioneering, innovative, and capable of undertaking key research tasks in the relevant fields; and their research results have brought about economic and social benefits. Since 2015, the researchers in the center have undertaken or participated in two major projects sponsored by the National Social Science Fund of China, two general projects sponsored by the National Social Science Fund of China, one subproject of the Innovation Project of the Chinese Academy of Social Sciences, and 11 provincial projects. These projects are not only significant for academic progress, but also meaningful for social and economic development as well as government decision-making. Among them there are “Research on the Current Development of the Situation in the Middle East and China’s Strategic Responses”, “Research on the Two-way Interaction Between Globalization and International Security”, “Investigation and Research on the Trade Development of the Enterprises from Anhui Province in the Member States of the West African Economic Community”, and “Investigation and Research on the Implementation of China’s ‘Belt and Road’ Initiative”. The center’s researchers, including part-time researchers, have published more than 50 papers in domestic and foreign academic journals (excluding results of special researches funded by enterprises, results of internal researches entrusted by local governments or enterprises, results published in internal journals, and the like), of which nearly 1/3 were published in journals of the Chinese Social Sciences Citation Index (CSSCI), exerting considerable academic influence.

In addition, the center strives to develop in-depth cooperation with other scientific research institutes, enterprises in relevant imdustries, local governments and foreign research institutions. It hires domestic scholars with rich experience and attainments in West Asian and African studies as consultants. Among them are Mr. Wu Sike, China’s former Special Envoy on Middle East Affairs; Professor Li Anshan, director of the Center for African Studies, Peking University; and Professor Liu Hongwu, director of the Institute of African Studies, Zhejiang Normal University. Besides, it hires a foreign expert, Professor Mongi Madini from the University of Franche-Comté of France, who specializes in language analysis, as a consultant.

The center has a General Office and three specialized research divisions, namely, the Division of Middle East Studies, the Division of African Studies, and the Division of Anhui-Asian and Anhui-African Economic Cooperation Studies. Research plans are formulated every year.

II. Contact Information

Website: http://yfyjzx.ahu.edu.cn/

Contact Person: Wang Zezhuang; Tel: +86-551-65108870; Email: wangzezhuang@126.com

Correspondence Address: Level 2, West Wing, Main Teaching Building, Anhui University (Longhe Campus), No. 3 Feixi Road, Hefei City, Anhui Province, P. R. China.

Department for Developing Countries Studies, China Institute of International Studies

I. Introduction

China Institute of International Studies is the first specialized institution of the People's Republic of China focusing on international studies, and was established on November 24, 1956. In 2017, the institute was selected as a candidate unit of China Top Think Tanks; and in 2020, it was approved as a pilot unit. The institute is also home to China's first research center for Xi Jinping Thought on Diplomacy. African studies are conducted in the Department for Developing Countries Studies of the institute, which was originally the Fourth Research Office, and then the Division for Developing Countries Studies, of China Department of International Studies. In 2014, as China Department of International Studies was renamed China Institute of International Studies, the Division for Developing Countries Studies was correspondingly transformed into the Department for Developing Countries Studies, which is one of the eight specialized departments of China Institute of

International Studies. African studies are a key research focus of the Department for Developing Countries Studies. The development goal of the institute is to build a first-level unit of China Top Think Tanks to serve the country's diplomacy, particularly its diplomacy with Africa. China Institute of International Studies has trained a large number of diplomatic talents for China, some of whom became Chinese ambassadors and senior diplomats to African countries. The journal of the institute *China International Studies* (Chinese and English editions) irregularly publishes research articles of domestic and foreign scholars on African region and China-Africa relations, exerting much influence at home and abroad.

The mission of the Department for Developing Countries Studies is to actively carry out research on international issues as well as track II diplomacy and public diplomacy in close cooperation with the government's work toward Africa. The researchers study Africa as well as its role and influence in global affairs from the perspectives of politics, economy, security and society; the relations between China and African countries so as to provide policy advisory for strengthening mutual assistance and cooperation between the countries; and hot issues related to Africa as well as their international impacts. In their research, macro studies are combined with regional and country-specific studies. China Institute of International Studies has professionals working in the Chinese embassies to African countries all year round, engaging in front-line diplomatic and research work. The Department for Developing Countries Studies currently has two researchers, three associate researchers, and five assistant researchers, and most of them have doctoral degrees.

Carrying out track II diplomacy and public diplomacy in close cooperation with the government is one of the important responsibilities of the institute, and therefore its international exchanges are quite frequent. Every year, the department receives a large number of experts, scholars and officials from Africa, as well as delegations of scholars and officials from European and American countries who are involved in African studies. The researchers of the department visit different countries of Africa several times a year for field researches and investigations.

II. Contact Information

Website: http://www.ciis.org.cn/

WeChat Official Account: CIIS_since_1956

Contact Person: Zeng Aiping; Tel: +86-10-85119580; Email: zengaiping@ciis.org.cn

Correspondence Address: No. 3 Toutiao, Taijichang, Dongcheng District, Beijing (100005), P. R. China.

Institute of West-Asian and African Studies Chinese Academy of Social Sciences (China-Africa Institute)

I. Introduction

To strengthen the research on Africa, in September 1959, the Publicity Department of the Central Committee of the Communist Party of China (CCCPC) entrusted the Division of Philosophy and Social Sciences of the Chinese Academy of Sciences, the predecessor of the Chinese Academy of Social Sciences (CASS), with setting up a preparatory team for the establishment of an Asian and African studies institute. On July 4, 1961, following Chairman Mao Zedong's instruction, the Institute of Asian and African Studies of the Chinese Academy of Sciences was officially established. On January 20, 1964, the institute was split into an Institute of West Asian and African Studies and an Institute of Southeast Asian Studies. On October 30, 1964, the institute was officially renamed the Institute of West-Asian and African Studies (IWAAS). On January 1, 1981, the IWAAS was put under the administration of the CASS. On September 3, 2018, President Xi Jinping announced the establishment of a China-Africa Institute at the 2018 Beijing Summit of the Forum on China-Africa Cooperation (FOCAC). On April 9, 2019, the China-Africa Institute was formally established on the basis of strong research strength of the CASS. Since then, the IWAAS and the China-Africa Institute have been operating in the form of "one faculty for two institutes", and are now China's largest academic institutions and top think tanks on West-Asian and African studies.

The IWAAS is a comprehensive and multidisciplinary academic institution, and China's academic center of West-Asian and African studies. Its research covers 71 West-Asian and African countries, and is mainly focused on contemporary political, economic, social, international relations, legal, ethnic, religious and other issues in the region. The IWAAS provides policy advisory for the CCCPC and the State Council, and consultancy services for relevant enterprises and institutions.

The IWAAS currently has over 70 research and management personnel, including 54 professional and technical personnel. Under the IWAAS are six research divisions, two editorial departments, an information center and a general office. The Division of Political Studies focuses its research on political development paths, political systems, party systems, political organizations, politicians, political development issues, legal systems, and legal regimes of the Middle East and Africa. The Division of Economic Studies focuses its research on economic development strategies, economic systems, economic policies and reforms, resources and markets, industrial structures and adjustments, and the regional integration process of the Middle East and Africa, as well as cooperative construction of the "Belt and Road" by China and Africa. The Division of International Relations Studies focuses its research on the relations between major powers and the Middle East and Africa, the relations among the countries in the region, the foreign relations of the countries in the region, the relations between China and the region, and important international organizations in the region. The Division of Social & Cultural Studies focuses its research on the history, social system, social structure, social issues, social governance, social security, forms of civilization, culture and education in the region. The Division of Ethnic and Religious Studies focuses its research on ethnic policies, relations, forms and issues of the region as well as traditional religions, Judaism, Christianity and Islam in the region. The Division of Security Studies focuses its research on regional and national security strategies, security mechanisms, security governance and security issues in the Middle East and Africa, as well as traditional and non-traditional security issues such as regional conflicts, counter-terrorism situations, and piracy issues in the region. The Editorial Departments edit and issue *West Asia and Africa* and *China-Africa Journal*, publishing papers on the history, politics, economy, international relations, society, culture, ethnicity and religion of the Middle East and Africa as well as papers on the relations between China and the region. The Information Center provides literature and information on the studies of the Middle East and Africa, and runs the institute's Chinese and English websites and WeChat official account, releasing important research results and information on the Middle East and Africa in time.

The IWAAS is a pioneer in Middle East and African research in China. It has gathered a large number of talents with profound accumulation and abundant achievements together, and played a leading role in the field of Middle East and African research in China, exerting considerable influence on the international community. Firstly, it boasts an overall advantage in disciplinary construction. The IWAAS has yielded systematic research achievements, both in fundamental research and applied research, with long-term accumulation and pioneering study efforts. Among them are *Handbook of Africa, Overview of Africa, Handbook of the Middle East, Concise Encyclopedia of West Asia and North Africa, Concise Encyclopedia of Africa* and multi-volume series of national chronicles, *Annual Report on Development in the Middle East and Africa, Annual Report on Development in the Middle East,* and *Annual Report on Development in Africa.* Meanwhile, there are a number of influential works in tertiary disciplines. All these works have great influence on the academic circle. Some of them are the foundation works of the discipline, and some of them have filled the gaps in domestic academic research. Secondly, it boasts a size advantage in the talent team. The institute gathers together a relatively large number of high-level talents specializing in Middle East and African research in China. They have high degrees, diverse disciplinary backgrounds, rich academic experience, broad research horizons, strong research capabilities, solid academic foundation, good professional quality and other outstanding characteristics. At present, the team features a reasonable age structure. More than 10 experts and young scholars have experience of working in the target country for many years and are familiar with the basic national conditions of the target country. All above makes the research strength of the IWASS advantageous over other research institutions of the same kind in China. Thirdly, it boasts a platform advantage in disciplinary development. (1) Important academic publicity platforms: two journals and four websites. Thanks to the core journal *West Asia and Africa* (since 1980), *China-Africa Journal* (since 2020) and four websites, the institute has gained considerable influence at home and abroad. (2) Domestic academic organizations and groups. The Chinese Society of Asian and African Studies and the Chinese Association of Middle East Studies are affiliated with the institute. The presidents and secretaries-general of both associations are staff members of the institute, thus providing important resources to lead the country's academic research on the Middle East and Africa. The establishment of the Gulf Research Center of the CASS and the Center of South African Studies provides important support for regional and country-specific studies. (3) High-end international platforms. The Asian Federation of Middle East Associations is an institutionalized and international academic platform initiated by the institute. It holds international seminars biennially. In 2018, a "China Studies Center" was established in the United Arab Emirates University to expand the academic influence. Fourthly, it boasts a foundation advantage in disciplinary development. In terms of the development of the "three major systems", the institute has been approved of one advantageous discipline and two key disciplines of the Summit Program of the CASS, and has established two key disciplines at the institute level. All of these have provided important support in both funds and staff for its disciplinary construction and development.

In terms of degree education, the University of Chinese Academy of Social Sciences (UCASS), particularly the Graduate School of the Chinese Academy of Social Sciences (GSCASS), has established the Department of West Asian and African Studies at the IWAAS, recruiting master's and doctoral students, and has set up a post-doctoral research station. The department offers three majors and six research directions: (1) World Economy, with the directions of Middle East Economy and African Economy; (2) International Politics, with the directions of Middle East Politics and African Politics; and (3) International Relations, with the directions of Middle East International Relations and African International Relations. The courses offered by the department cover multiple aspects of the Middle East and Africa, including politics, economy, international relations, history, and social culture. The department strives to mentor comprehensive talents with solid professional knowledge as well as scientific and systematic research methods. Since 1978, it has trained about 70 master's and doctoral students.

The establishment of the China-Africa Institute has injected new momentum into the development of the IWAAS. The China-Africa Institute aims to gather resources from academic think tanks in China and Africa, deepen mutual learning of Chinese and African civilizations, strengthen exchanges of governance and development experience, brainstorm ideas and suggestions for China-Africa cooperation as well as the cooperation of China and Africa with other countries, and enhance mutual understanding and friendship between Chinese and African people. It seeks to provide intellectual and talent support for the cooperation among the "Belt and Road" countries, joint building of a future-oriented comprehensive strategic and cooperative China-Africa partnership, and joint building of a closer China-Africa community with a shared future. The China-Africa Institute has studied and implemented the spirit of the congratulatory letter from President Xi Jinping to its establishment, vigorously promoting the development of the "three major systems", striving to bring into full play the "four major functions", and strengthening the building of an academic top think tank. Firstly, bring into play the role of the exchange platform and intensify academic exchanges between China and Africa. The institute is determined to well host "Africa Forum", "China Forum", and "Ambassadors' Forum", well run the "China-Africa Exchange Mechanism on Governance", the "China-Africa Exchange Mechanism on Sustainable Development" and the "China-

Africa Exchange Mechanism on Joint Construction of the ‘Belt and Road’”, and host “China-Africa Civilization Dialogue”, “China-Africa Think Tank Forum” and other high-end seminars. Secondly, bring into play the role of the research base and focus the research on the joint construction of the “Belt and Road”. The institute is determined to carry out studies of China-Africa cooperation, release 50 research topics every three years, follow up research on hot issues of common concern between the two parties, and successively launch the “Collections of the China-Africa Institute”, covering the aspects of think tank reports, academic monographs, research theses, classic translations, legal translations and yearbooks. Thirdly, bring into play the role of the talent high ground and mentor high-end professional talents. The institute is determined to provide academic degree education and promote such projects as exchange visits between Chinese and African scholars and high-end talent training. Fourthly, bring into play the role of the publicity window and tell the story of China-Africa friendship well. The institute is determined to run the Chinese and English websites of the China-Africa Institute well and establish the internationalized and specialized research publication *Journal of China-Africa Studies* in Chinese, English and French.

The current leaders include Cai Fang, president of the China-Africa Institute; Li Xinfeng, general-director of the IWAAS and executive vice-president of the China-Africa Institute; Guo Hong, party secretary of the IWAAS and vice-president of the China-Africa Institute; and Wang Lincong, secretary of the Committee for Discipline Inspection and deputy director-general of the IWAAS and vice-president of the China-Africa Institute.

II. Contact Information

Website:http://iwaas.cass.cn/ (IWAAS) http://cai.cssn.cn/ (China-Africa Institute)

WeChat Official Account: China_Africa2019

Contact Person: Ma Junwei; Tel: +86-10-87421055

Correspondence Address: China-Africa Institute, No. 1 National Stadium North Road, Chaoyang District, Beijing (100101), P. R. China.

Asia-Africa Development Research Institute of Development Research Center of the State Council, P.R.C.

I. Introduction

The Asia-Africa Development Research Institute of the Development Research Center of the State Council, P.R.C. (AADRI) was established on January 18, 1994. In accordance with the requirements of the CCCPC on the building of a new-type think tank with Chinese characteristics, under the leadership of the Development Research Center of the State Council, P.R.C., adhering to the core value of "seeking truth from facts, upholding integrity and bringing forth new ideas", meeting the need of modernization of the national governance system and governance capacity, and persisting in the approach of integrating theory with practice, the institute carries out objective and rational research on the relations among the countries of Asia and Africa, domestic and foreign policies and development strategies of individual countries in the region, and regional hot issues and emergencies, and provides policy advisory and consultancy services for national decision-making departments and relevant institutions.

The Department of Africa is an internal institution of the AADRI specializing in African development studies and provides high-quality intellectual support for the central government's scientific decision-making on China-Africa relations and Africa-related issues. In 2004, the AADRI established *Asia and Africa Review (bimonthly)*, issuing policy-related, strategic and academic articles, with the Department of Africa responsible for the Africa-related column. (In May 2015, in response to the development of the situation and the changes in the needs of the central government, *Asia and Africa Review* was renamed *Asia-Pacific Security and Maritime Affairs*.) In March 2013, the AADRI established its website to publicize related academic exchange activities, research results and Asian-African hot issues, with the Department of Africa responsible for the operation and maintenance of the website pages on Africa. In March of the same year, the AADRI established the Overseas Interests Research Center, with the Department of Africa responsible for in-depth investigations on Africa-related events, in an attempt to provide specialized research and consultancy services for the protection of China's interests in Africa and the entry of Chinese enterprises into Africa.

For a long time, the Department of Africa has closely followed up and deeply conducted research on African major political, economic and social issues that the national and relevant government departments are concerned about. It has trained some research backbones, built up a research team composed of full-time and guest researchers, and made a number of fruitful achievements. These achievements not only provided important and useful intellectual support for policy-making, which reflects its role as a think tank for the government, but also effectively promoted cooperation and exchanges between domestic and foreign institutions of African studies. It also provided support through publications and websites for professionals specializing in African issues and all sectors of society to track changes in Africa, deeply understand Africa and conduct research on African issues.

II. Contact Information

Website:http://www.aadrc.org.cn/

Contact Person: Li Bo; Tel: +86-10-68745141; Fax: +86-10-68745697; Email: hasann@126.com

Correspondence Address: East Wing, Level 5, No. 61 Zhichun Road, Haidian District, Beijing (100190), P. R. China.

Center for African Studies, Peking University

I. Introduction

The Center for African Studies at Peking University is an interdisciplinary and comprehensive research institution integrating teaching, scientific research, policy advisory and talent mentoring. It consists of teachers and research fellows from different departments and institutes of the university. Formerly known as the Asia-Africa Institute (engaged in both research and teaching) and led by

Mr. Ji Xianlin, it has become an important center for Asian, African and Latin American research in China since the early 1960s. Relying on the highly competitive faculties from the Asian, African and Latin American Academic Group of the Department of History, the Department of Oriental Languages and Literature, the Department of Western Languages and Literature, the Department of Political Science, the Department of Philosophy and Religion, and the Department of Sociology, the institute has been continuously playing a role of leading the domestic research on African history and current situation, and mentoring specialized talents. In 1998, when African studies in China were at the low point, Lu Tingen, He Fangchuan, ZhengJiaxin and other senior scholars proposed the establishment of the first center for African studies in China to gather together the advantageous resources of all disciplines of the university to conduct multi-disciplinary and comprehensive research on Africa. So far, the center has trained multiple professional talents for other universities and think tanks in China, and yielded a wealth of research results on African history and current situation. It is the earliest center of African studies established by a university in China and one of the three earliest regional and country-specific research centers of Peking University. The center now has about 20 research personnel from different departments of Peking University and 14 guest research fellows. The main advantages of the center lie in the joint participation of multiple disciplines and departments, and its wider research fields than other universities. Meanwhile, as the President Unit of the Chinese Society of African Historical Studies, the center also plays a role in uniting scholars of the whole country specializing in African studies, and maintaining close communication and cooperation with related government departments and business people. It is committed to leading and promoting African studies in China.

The center has three major goals: (1) to gradually establish some necessary databases and collect searchable materials so that the personnel doing practical work can easily find related materials; (2) to provide reference and consultancy services for some practical programs so as to truly suit the methods to the situation on the basis of in-depth investigations; and (3) to carry out people-to-people and social exchanges as well as cooperative research with think tanks at home and abroad, especially with those in Africa.

The center has three major tasks: (1) The center actively serves national policies and social needs. It not only focuses on fundamental research, but also provides support for the national development strategy by offering consultancy services for China-Africa cooperation and exchanges. In the past two years, it has made great contributions in consultancy services. (2) The center attaches great importance to the training of Chinese students and talents from Africa. It not only trains scarce talents, such as talents in African language and literature and in China-African relations, but also mentors multidisciplinary and comprehensive research talents through interdisciplinary course selection and other initiatives. Meanwhile, it also participates in the training of a large number of African degree students (undergraduates, masters and doctors) and non-degree students every year. (3) In addition to teaching and research, the center pays special attention to cultural exchanges between China and Africa, and plays a role in promoting exchanges and interactions between Chinese and African personnel. It not only hosts academic lectures, forums, and African activity weeks, but also organizes and coordinates activities including those on African literature and drama performances, providing opportunities for African students in Beijing and African personnel in China (from the political, cultural and academic circles) to integrate with Chinese academic and cultural communities.

The center has made three special achievements: (1) The center publishes *PKU-African-Tele-Info* (weekly), which has 6,000 readers including important government officials as well as scholars and social figures at home and abroad, and has become an important window with strong credibility for African studies in China. (2) The "BOYA Forum of Peking University on Africa" held by the center every year has also become a well-known forum for African studies in China. (3) Since 2011, the center has published the *Annual Review of African Studies in China* every year and invited domestic and foreign research fellows to share their opinions so as to promote African research in China.

II. Contact Information

Website: https://caspu.pku.edu.cn/

WeChat Official Account: Pkucas

Contact Person: Xu Liang; Tel: +86-10-62751632

Correspondence Address: School of International Studies, Peking University, No. 5 Yiheyuan Road, Haidian District, Beijing (100871), P. R. China.

Research and Development Department of China-Africa Development Fund

I. Introduction

The establishment of the China-Africa Development Fund (CADFund) is an important measure announced by the Chinese government at the FOCAC Beijing Summit in 2006, aiming to provide encouragement and support for Chinese enterprises to invest in Africa. The CADFund was officially launched in June 2007, with planned capital of five billion US dollars. At the FOCAC Johannesburg Summit held in December 2015, President Xi Jinping announced that, in order to support the implementation of the "Ten Major Plans for China-Africa Cooperation", the capital of the fund will be increased by five billion US dollars and thus reaches a total amount of 10 billion US dollars. In September 2018, President Xi Jinping put forward the "Eight Major Actions" in the keynote speech at the opening ceremony of the FOCAC Beijing Summit. In the first plan of "Industry Promotion", he emphasized to continue to bring the CADFund into play. Thc CADFund is China's first equity investment fund specializing in Africa and has played an important role in guiding and supporting Chinese enterprises' investment in Africa.

The Research and Development Department of the CADFund specializes in research related to investment in Africa. Since its establishment in 2008, the department has kept conducting studies in the aspects of "African Development" and 'China-Africa Cooperation", and has gradually formed a brand of African research think tank focusing on investment in Africa. The research results have provided intellectual support for national policy-making, fund business and cooperative enterprises, gaining a good reputation in the industry.

The main achievements of the Research and Development Department are as follows: It has undertaken more than ten projects commissioned by the Office of the Central Leading Group on Financial and Economic Affairs, the National Development and Reform Commission, the Ministry of Foreign Affairs, and the Ministry of Commerce. It has also submitted consultancy analyses and advices, many of which were adopted by the General Office of the CCCPC, the General Office of the State Council, the Research Office of the State Council, the National Academy of Governance, and the Xinhua News Agency. Its country-specific studies cover 54 African countries and provide comprehensive and original analyses for investment in different countries. Its industry research focuses on key areas of investment in Africa and provides market analysis, data information and strategic advices. It focuses on hot, difficult and key issues related to investment in Africa as well as management mechanisms and business models of peer institutions to provide specialized analysis. In addition, it monitors global political and economic situation as well as hot issues and market and industrial trends in Africa, and provides two consultancy products, namely, *African Daily* and *Political and Economic Situation Analysis Weekly*. As of March 2020, nearly 3,000 issues of *African Daily* and 400 issues of *Political and Economic Situation Analysis Weekly* have been published.

II. Contact Information

Website: http://www.cadfund.com/

Contact Person: Xu Zelai; Tel: +86-10-59892982; Email: xuzelai@cadfund.com

Correspondence Address: Level 11, East Tower, Chemsunny World Trade Center, No. 28 Fuxingmennei Street, Xicheng District, Beijing (100031), P. R. China.

China Africa Industrial Forum Expert Committee

I. Introduction

The China Africa Industrial Forum Expert Committee was established in November 2009 and is a brainpower team consisting of professionals from different fields related to China and Africa, including envoys of African countries to China, former Chinese ambassadors to African countries, representatives of international organizations, leaders of national ministries and commissions, and famous scholars in the studies of China and Africa.

The committee is the guiding institution for the China Africa Industrial Forum to conduct various activities. It provides suggestions and opinions on the cooperation and exchanges between China and Africa in economy, culture, science and technology, regularly publishes academic reports on hot topics related to China and Africa, and formulates strategic plans for Chinese enterprises' investment and development in Africa.

The main activities of the committee include the following four aspects: (1) academic exchanges: holding valuable academic and small-sized professional seminars on a regular basis; (2) guest discussions: inviting Chinese and African officials, scholars and well-known experts of different field to jointly discuss and analyze hot topics related to China and Africa as well as the direction and methods of mutual cooperation and exchanges with the members of the committee; (3) consultancy and guidance: through communication with Chinese enterprises, formulating tailor-made strategic plans for these enterprises in terms of operation, management and technology to help them enter the African market; and (4) research reports: releasing the *Index Report on the Prospect of African Industrialization* and the *Index Report on the African Business Environment* every year.

What's more, the Annual Seminar of African Experts held by the committee since its establishment has become an important indicator for all sectors of society to learn more about Africa. The *Index Report on the Prospect of African Industrialization* and the *Index Report on the African Business Environment* have become important reference materials for Chinese enterprises to invest and trade in Africa.

The committee organizes experts and scholars to visit Africa for field exchanges and research every year. In just 10 years, they visited more than 30 countries and held exchanges and discussions with over 100 organizations, and won support from all walks of life in Africa and praise from local institutions.

In the future, the committee will mainly focus its research on African industrialization, investment, trade and business environment, and strive to become a credible research institution for Chinese enterprises' entry into Africa.

II. Contact Information

Website: http://www.zfhz.org/

WeChat Official Account: CAIF_zfhz

Contact Person: Lyu Bin; Email: www.caif_zf-hz@163.com

Correspondence Address: Room 11M, Duhui International, No. A3 Shilipu, Chaoyang District, Beijing, P. R. China.

Africa Studies Center of China Foreign Affairs University

I. Introduction

The Africa Studies Center of China Foreign Affairs University (CFAU), which was founded in December 2009, is a non-profit mass academic organization affiliated with CFAU. In 2017, it was approved as a Regional and Country-Specific Studies Center Registered with the Ministry of Education. The first director of the center was Professor Tang Xiao (2009-2016), and the second director was Professor Li Dan (2016- 2019). Both professors successively served as members of the Steering Committee of the China-Africa Joint Research and Exchange Program of the Ministry of Foreign Affairs. The center is non-physical and its members come from various departments and research centers of CFAU, including the Department of Diplomacy and Foreign Affairs Management, the Department of English & International Studies, the Department of Foreign

Languages, the Department of International Law, the Department of International Economics, and the Institute of Asian Studies, featuring diverse background.

The mission of the center is to actively conduct academic research and exchanges on political, economic and cultural relations between China and African countries, promote teaching and research of CFAU related to Africa, and serve the government's scientific decision-making.

The main activities of the center include publishing research papers and monographs on Africa and China-Africa relations, undertaking research programs, enhancing students' understanding of Africa, fostering their doctoral dissertations and master's theses on Africa and China-Africa relations, and writing research reports for relevant government departments. Up till now, it has completed more than ten programs on African studies. Among them are "Research on the Formation Mechanism and Evolutionary Rules of China's National Image in Africa", "Research on the Feasibility and Operation Mode of China's Construction of a Regional Logistics Center in Africa", "African Leaders' Third Term Phenomenon and its Impact", "Research on China-Gabon Relations Under the Framework of China-Africa Comprehensive Strategic Cooperative Partnership", "New Trends in Diplomatic Philosophy and Institutional Reform of France", "Research on International Cooperation in the Development of African Information and Communications Industry and China-Africa Cooperation Strategy", "Research on the Risks Faced by Chinese-Invested Enterprises in Africa and Coping Strategies from the Perspective of Game Theory".

In terms of international exchanges, CFAU signed a memorandum of understanding with the Foreign Service Institute of Kenya and the Moroccan Academy of Diplomatic Studies. In 2012, the Africa Studies Center of CFAU applied for and successfully joined the "China-Africa Think Tanks 10+10 Partnership Plan". As a result, it has formed a partnership with the International Relations Institute of Cameroon and become one of the top ten domestic centers of African studies that have established academic exchange partnerships with African academies. It has undertaken multiple academic exchange projects of the China-

Africa Joint Research and Exchange Program of the Ministry of Foreign Affairs to receive scholars from Francophone countries of Africa, with the themes of African security situation and China-Africa security cooperation, African countries' exploration of development paths suitable for their own national conditions, and promotion of the building of a closer China-Africa community with a shared future. In addition, the center has invited scholars from African universities and research institutions to CFAU for short-term visits.

The development goal of the center is to carry out in-depth fundamental research, especially on Ethiopia, Eritrean, Gabon, Gambia, Ghana, Guinea and Guinea-Bissau; regularize exchange visits and cooperative research with African universities and research institutions; regularly hold African research seminars; and yield high-quality research results and consultancy reports.

II. Contact Information

Website: http://fzzx.cfau.edu.cn/

Contact Person: Wu Mengru; Tel: +86-10-68323114; Email: wumengru@cfau.edu.cn

Correspondence Address: Scientific Research Office, China Foreign Affairs University, No. 24 Zhanlanguan Road, Xicheng District, Beijing (100037), P. R. China.

Africa Communication Research Center, Communication University of China

I. Introduction

Founded on December 10, 2012, the Africa Communication Research Center at the Communication University of China (CUC) is the first institute of African media research in China. The center aims to build a high-end academic platform between China and Africa for communication research and talent mentoring in the 21st century. Since its establishment, the center has forged ahead in three major fields, namely, scientific research, personnel cultivation, and people-to-people exchanges between China and Africa, and has become an institute of Africa-related studies with distinctive characteristics.

Relying on the advantages of the university, the center focuses on research in China-Africa communication-related fields. The members of the center have conducted a series of studies on such topics as the building of China's national image and power of speech in Africa, big data research on African public opinions about China, public diplomacy and media cooperation between China and Africa, media development in Africa, and comparative research on media communication between China and Africa. They have undertaken national and provincial scientific research projects multiple times, producing a number of representative research results and consultancy reports. They have undertaken and completed the project "Research on China's Image and Influence in African Countries" sponsored by the National Social Science Fund of China. They have also undertaken multiple research projects of the "China-Africa Joint Research and Exchange Program" of the Ministry of Foreign Affairs, conducting research on China's public diplomacy to Africa, China's media communication strategy in Africa, African media development, and China's discourse communication strategy in Africa. In addition, the center has undertaken key projects related to Africa entrusted by the Cyberspace Administration of China, the Ministry of Culture and Tourism, and other ministries and commissions. In the research field of China's communication to Africa, a number of papers, in Chinese and English, have been published. Among them, Professor Zhang Yanqiu's exposition of China's communication to Africa centering around "constructive news" has aroused the attention and discussion of African, European and American academic circles and media, and has been reported by the British Broadcasting Corporation (BBC), China Global Television Network (CGTN), China Daily and multiple African media.

Since its establishment, the center has concretely promoted China's communication, education and training in Africa. The center plays an active role in Africa-related media training projects of the Ministry of Commerce, and has trained a number of African journalists and information officers who are familiar with and amicable to China. The CUC has undertaken the project of the Ministry of Commerce for training masters of international communication for developing countries since 2011, and the staff of the Africa Communication Research Center have shouldered lots of management and teaching tasks in it. The project has cultivated more than 200 senior journalists and information officers from more than 60 developing countries. Among them, two-thirds were Africans from nearly 30 countries in Africa. When they returned to their home countries after graduation, they became influential information officers, media professionals, and scholars specializing in China-Africa communication studies, including the press officer of the Office of the President of South Africa, the director of the Office of the Vice President of South Sudan, counselors of African embassies and consulates in other countries, media directors, anchors of national television stations, and reporters of well-known media. The photo of the graduation ceremony of the project was selected into the large-scale achievement exhibition of "Five Years of Hard Work" before the 19th National Congress of the Communist Party of China (CPC). In addition, the staff of the center have taught several courses and participated in receptions for African journalists training projects undertaken by the Ministry of Commerce, the China Foreign Languages Publishing Administration, and the National Radio and Television Administration. The number of trainees reached 1,000, which helped African journalists renewed their opinions on China-related media, and made them more familiar with and more amicable to China.

The center has established sound relationships with African universities and research institutions, and has become a platform for people-to-people exchanges with fruitful results in the field of media research between China and Africa. It has established stable and active exchange relations with key universities in South Africa, Kenya, Ethiopia, Nigeria, Ghana, Egypt, Zimbabwe, Zambia, Malawi, South Sudan and other countries, carrying out media project studies, personnel exchanges, paper reviews, joint publications and other activities. The CUC signed school-level memorandums of cooperation with the University of the

Witwatersrand, the Rhodes University, Seijoh-University, the British University of Egypt, Zanzibar National University and other universities, and jointly launched the project of "China-Africa Report" with the School of Journalism and the School of Media Studies of the Witwatersrand University of South Africa. From 2017 to 2019, the center has been entrusted by the Ministry of Foreign Affairs for three consecutive years with the African scholars' and journalists' visit project of the "China-Africa Joint Research and Exchange Program", and has received more than 60 scholars of media studies from well-known African universities, think tank personnel, and famous media practitioners for short-term exchanges in China, which has promoted exchanges between Chinese and African scholars of media studies. The research backbones of the center have visited Africa multiple times, actively participated in international seminars related to Africa and disseminated Chinese academic propositions.

At the end of 2019, the center was incorporated into the scientific research strategic platform directly under the university—the Institute of Community of Shared Future for Mankind. Meanwhile, China's first African media think tank—"CUC-Star Times African Media Joint Research Think Tank" was established. The establishment of the joint think tank is a strong-strong cooperation between the CUC and Star Times in the field of Africa-related media research and media market development, and is of great significance in promoting China-Africa economic and trade cooperation and people-to-people exchanges under the "Belt and Road" Initiative. The African Media Research Center will actively work on the building of a community with a shared future for mankind, build on past achievements and strive for new progresses, and earnestly promote the dissemination and development of the awareness of China-Africa community with a shared future.

II. Contact Information

Website:http://www.icsf.cuc.edu.cn/

WeChat Official Account: gh_b7741c0d26fd

Contact Person: Zhang Yanqiu; Email: yqzhang@cuc.edu.cn

Correspondence Address: Room 112, Building 42, Communication University of China, No. 1, Dingfuzhuang East Street, Chaoyang District, Beijing (100024), P. R. China.

Institute of African Studies, School of Foreign Studies, University of International Relations

I. Introduction

The Institute of African Studies at the School of Foreign Languages in the University of International Relations, officially established in 2013, is a physical entity of African regional and country-specific studies. Based on China's current policy toward Africa and its overall development strategy, the institute focuses on the history, politics, society and culture of African countries, especially Francophone countries of Africa, and studies the relations between China and Africa, France and Africa, as well as other European and American countries and Africa, with a view to providing theoretical guidance, academic analysis and consultancy services for China's policy toward Africa, cultural exchanges between China and Africa, and non-governmental economic and trade exchanges.

The main body of the researchers consists of the teachers of the Department of French Language of the University of International Relations. The institute hires professionals from the Department of International Politics, the Department of International Economics, the Department of Culture and Communication, and the Department of Law, as well as off-campus professionals in African studies as part-time researchers to form an interdisciplinary research team. It also hires well-known experts with high reputation, outstanding academic achievements, and concerns and support for African research as consultants, and hires professionals worldwide with rich experience and knowledge of African local conditions as guest researchers.

The institute has forged sound exchange and cooperation mechanisms with institutions, professionals, publishers and think tanks in African studies at home and abroad, including China Institutes of Contemporary International Relations, the Institute of West-Asian and African Studies of the Chinese Academy of Social Sciences, the Institute of African Studies of Zhejiang Normal University, making it advantageous in information sharing, thinking collision and academic interaction.

Since the establishment of the institute, the researchers have actively participated in major seminars on African studies at home and abroad, and have visited Africa to conduct field investigations. Up to now, they have led or participated in the projects related to the protection of China's overseas interests, China-Africa cooperation in "non-traditional security", China-Africa security situation, and relations between China and Francophone countries of Africa. Among them are "Contemporary Cultural Strategies of France Toward Francophone Countries of West Africa" of the "China-Africa Joint Research and Exchange Program" of the Ministry of Foreign Affairs, the "African Media" column in *African Regional Development Report 2014-2015* of the Ministry of Education, as well as "Translation and Research of Contemporary African French Literature and Afro-French Literature", "Research on African Factors in China-French Relations", and "Prospects and Problems of China-Africa Exchanges and Cooperation—Taking African Immigrants Held Up in Guangzhou as an Example" of the African Research Base of Zhejiang Normal University.

The institute will take the establishment of the China-Africa comprehensive strategic partnership as a historical opportunity to explore new ideas and new approaches for China-Africa friendly exchanges, and make contributions to joint realization of the "Chinese Dream" and the "African Dream".

II. Contact Information

Website: https://waiyuxueyuan.uir.cn/ysjg/fzyjs/

Contact Person: Liu Tiannan; Tel: +86-10-62861354; Email: violine505@163.com

Correspondence Address: No. 12 Poshangcun, Haidian District, Beijing (100091), P. R. China.

Institute of African Studies, China Institutes of Contemporary International Relations

I. Introduction

China Institutes of Contemporary International Relations (CICIR), established in 1980, is one of the first pilot units of China Top Think Tanks. The Institute of African Studies was formerly a part of the Institute of West Asian and African Studies of CICIR. To meet the needs of the new development of China-Africa relations, CICIR established the Institute of African Studies in 2013 to conduct policy research and academic studies on Africa, especially on sub-Saharan Africa. Its research covers individual countries, African integration, major countries' policies towards Africa, and China-Africa relations. The research team is of a reasonable structure, including researchers, associate researchers and assistant researchers.

The Institute of African Studies maintains close ties with major academic research institutions in China. It has established communication mechanisms with more than 30 think tanks and universities in Africa, Europe and the United States, and receives dozens of foreign visitors every year. In 2018, it hosted a large-scale international academic conference titled "CICIR Forum 2018: China and Africa Jointly Building a Community of Shared Future for Mankind". As a member of the "China-Africa Think Tanks 10+10 Partnership Plan" under the FOCAC framework, the Institute of African Studies has become an exchange partner with the Institute of Security Studies of South Africa.

II. Contact Information

Website: http://www.cicir.ac.cn/

Contact Person: Sun Hong; Tel: +86-10-88547368; Email: sunhong@cicir.ac.cn

Correspondence Address: Institute of African Studies, China Institutes of Contemporary International Relations, No. A2 Wanshou Temple, Haidian District, Beijing (100081), P. R. China.

Center for Middle East and African Studies, Renmin University of China

I. Introduction

In 2013, the Chinese government put forward the "Belt and Road" Initiative, providing a large amount of investment for infrastructure construction to promote the development of the region along the "Silk Road". In view of the fact that the Middle East and Africa play key roles in the implementation of the "Belt and Road" Initiative, the Renmin University of China gathered experts and scholars from China, the Middle East and Africa, and officially established the Center for Middle East and African Studies in 2014 under the support of Sino-Israel Global Network & Academic Leadership, with the goal of cooperating to promote effective development of geo-economics and geopolitics in the region and helping people learn more about the complex situation of the region.

The center is committed to promoting the academic circle's understanding of the Middle East and Africa, including the development of regional relations and the prospect of hot issues, and aims to promote effective interaction between scholars of China and those of the Middle East and Africa, and provide a platform for cross-regional academic exchanges and cooperation.

The core objectives of the center include encouraging new and rational international cooperative research that can meet regional challenges, providing funds for Chinese scholars to attend international conferences in the Middle East and Africa, enhancing academic exchanges between China and related countries, and promoting in-depth mutual understanding and regional stability to fulfil its due function as a think tank.

At present, the center has altogether 12 full-time and part-time researchers, with professor Liu Qingjian as the director and associate professor Cui Shoujun as the executive director.

II. Contact Information

Contact Person: Cui Shoujun; Email: cuishoujun@hotmail.com

Correspondence Address: School of International Relations, Renmin University of China, No. 59 Zhongguancun Street, Haidian District, Beijing (100872), P. R. China.

Institute of West-Asian and African Studies, Chinese Academy of International Trade and Economic Cooperation, Ministry of Commerce

I. Introduction

The Chinese Academy of International Trade and Economic Cooperation (CAITEC) is a public institution directly under the Ministry of Commerce, and a comprehensive and multi-functional social science research and consultancy institution integrating economic and trade research, information consultation, press and publication, and education and training. It grew out of the Chinese Institute of International Economy founded in Hong Kong in August 1948, which moved to Guangzhou after the founding of the People's Republic of China in October 1949, and then moved to Beijing at the end of 1951. After institutional integrations in 1997 and 2002, the institute developed into today's CAITEC. Over the past seven decades, the CAITEC has been practical and active, and played a positive role in the development of China's commerce, gaining a high reputation at home and abroad. The CAITEC boasts a research and consultancy team of young people with senior titles, advanced degrees and professional expertise. Presently, more than 110 of them are senior professional and technical personnel, over 120 personnel have postgraduate qualifications or above, over 30 personnel enjoy special allowances from the State Council, and dozens of staff are working in China's overseas business organizations and international institutions.

The Institute of West-Asian and African Studies is one of the research units under the CAITEC. It was affiliated with the Institute of Asian and African Studies of the CAITEC and became independent in 2016. It is committed to the research on economic and trade relations between China and West Asian and African countries, cooperation and development relations between China and West Asian and African regional integration organizations, cooperation on production capacity between China and West Asian and African countries, and cooperation on the "Belt and Road" Initiative. It conducts continuous studies on economic development, key industries, economic and trade relations, and investment environment of West Asian and African countries as well as comprehensive, economic, trade, key and hot issues in the region. It provides consultancy services on economic and trade cooperation for the CCCPC, the State Council, national ministries and commissions including the Ministry of Commerce, and local governments and enterprises.

There are three departments under the institute, namely, the West Asia and North Africa Department, the Eastern Africa Department and the Southern Africa Department. The incumbent director of the institute is Mr. Zhang Jianping. There are altogether eight researchers, among whom seven have doctoral or post-doctorate degrees and deputy senior titles or above. Representative research achievements of the institute include serial annual reports of *China-Africa Economic and Trade Relations* as well as publications directly supporting the 2018 FOCAC Beijing Summit, including *2015-2018 Review of China-Africa Economic and Trade Cooperation Achievements, Study on the Policy of Expanding China's Import from Africa, New Trend of African Development and Its Impact on China-Africa Cooperation, Development Experience of Dubai Free Trade Zone and Its Implications for China.* All of these have accelerated China's studies on Africans economy, promoted China-Africa economic and trade cooperation, and provided intellectual support for the construction of the "Belt and Road".

The institute actively undertakes personnel cultivation tasks of the Graduate School of the CAITEC, and is committed to cultivating high-quality, high-level and interdisciplinary talents with international vision and solid theoretical attainment. 17 students have graduated with master's degrees in economics or finance. One doctoral student and nine postgraduate students are currently studying at the institute.

The researchers of the institute have been engaged in international exchanges. They attended and addressed high-level conferences on China-Africa cooperation in Morocco, Uganda, Tanzania, Ethiopia, Senegal and other countries. They have held Track 1.5 or Track 2 dialogues with the UK, the US, Germany, Australia and other developed countries on third-party cooperation in Africa. They have published articles and given interviews on China-Africa cooperation in the People's Daily, CCTV, CGTN and other media. By participating in international exchanges on China-Africa economy and trade and sharing research results, they have contributed their opinions on in-depth African studies and China-Africa cooperation.

II. Contact Information

Website: http://www.caitec.org.cn/

Contact Person: Han Zhuping; Tel: +86-10-64515187; Email: victoria.han.zhuping@outlook.com

Correspondence Address: No. 28 Donghouxiang, Andingmenwai Street, Dongcheng District, Beijing, P. R. China.

Center for African Studies, Beijing Foreign Studies University

I. Introduction

The Center for African Studies at Beijing Foreign Studies University (BFSU), founded in 2017, is a university-level center and a Regional and Country-Specific Studies Center Registered with the Ministry of Education. On September 23, 2019, the School of Asian and African Studies of BFSU was expanded and split into the School of Asian Studies and the School of African studies. After the adjustment of the management system, the Center for African Studies is now run by the School of African Studies.

The main research areas of the center are literature, linguistics, history and politics of Africa, China-Africa relations and so on. Since its establishment, the center has yielded some achievements in African languages, literature, and regional and country-specific studies. By virtue of its own characteristics, the research team actively explores translation and evaluation of African research results in Africa, China-Africa educational and cultural exchanges, and the relationship between African countries and the rest of the world. The project "Research on the Evolution of Native Literature in Hausa and Swahili During the British Colonial Period (1900-1960)", sponsored by the National Social Science Fund of China and led by Professor Sun Xiaomeng, is the flagship of the center.

There are now nine researchers at the center. Meanwhile, the center is working to play its role in integrating talents of African studies throughout the university, establishing an innovative interdisciplinary group with middle-aged and young teachers as the backbone, bringing into full play the strength of foreign experts, and carrying out cross-university cooperation in research. It has set up an open research team welcoming experts and scholars in and out of the university to join its projects as part-time or distinguished guest researchers.

With the multilingual and multidisciplinary platform provided by BFSU, the center will further conduct fundamental research, carry out countermeasure research in a targeted manner, and give full play to its social service function.

II. Contact Information

WeChat Official Account: bfsusas

Contact Person: Li Hongfeng; Email: lihongfeng@bfsu.edu.cn

Correspondence Address: No. 333 Main Building, East Campus, School of African Studies, Beijing Foreign Studies University, Beijing (100089), P. R. China.

Center for African Studies, Beijing Language and Culture University

I. Introduction

The Center for African Studies at Beijing Language and Culture University (BLCU), founded in 2017 and officially inaugurated in May, 2018, is a Regional and Country-Specific Studies Center Registered with the Ministry of Education.

It aims to build an information sharing platform for China-Africa cooperation and exchanges under the guidance of the "Belt and Road" Initiative and the principle of "enhancing China-Africa friendship and serving China-Africa cooperation".

Relying on its research strength and taking the need for talents specialized in French in the context of China-Africa cooperation as an opportunity, the Center for African Studies of the BLCU set up the course of "Studies on French-Speaking Countries and Regions" in March 2019, and the course has been included in the list of compulsory courses for postgraduate students majoring in French. The course is based on the teaching practice of "Studies on French-Speaking Countries and Regions" in France and around the world, and includes both theoretical and practical aspects. At the end of the semester, students are asked to write papers related to African studies according to their own interests and specialties. The center focuses its efforts on the mentoring of postgraduate students majoring in French who are willing to conduct African studies, and includes these students in the French specialist mentoring program, which aims to serve China-Africa cooperation. Based on the research platform for the faculty, the center organizes the students to regularly participate in relevant seminars, data collection and drafting of country-specific reports, discussions about regional and country-specific theories, investigations and questionnaires of regional and country-specific research projects, and other activities.

The plans for future studies and development of the center are: (1) to increase the proportion of professional knowledge such as the language, culture and society of target countries in the curriculum of undergraduate and postgraduate students majoring in French; (2) to carry out regional and country-specific studies among undergraduate and postgraduate students with language as the tool and theories of regional and country-specific studies as the key; (3) to establish the interactive learning mode of "target country students in China + Chinese undergraduate students majoring in French" by virtue of the resources of target country students in China to deepen understanding of each other and research on the social situation of target countries; (4) to establish long-term and stable relations with the embassies of target countries in China, and build emotional bonds for academic and cultural exchanges; (5) to establish close cooperation with Confucius Institutes in Francophone countries of Africa to widen channels for in-depth understanding of French-speaking target countries in Africa; and (6) to carry out field investigations in Frenching-speaking countries in Africa, build "teacher + student" academic communities, establish academic contact with local universities and hold lectures and seminars for each other.

II. Contact Information

Website: http://irs.blcu.edu.cn/col/col16046/index.html/

Contact Person: Li Yan; Tel: +86-10-82303514; Email: connie_liyan@163.com

Correspondence Address: Room 321, Teaching Building 5, Beijing Language and Culture University, No. 15 Xueyuan Road, Haidian District, Beijing (100083), P. R. China.

Tunisia Studies Center, University of International Business and Economics

I. Introduction

The Tunisia Studies Center at the University of International Business and Economics (UIBE) was established in March 2017 and afterwards approved as a Regional and Country-Specific Studies Center Registered with the Ministry of Education. In June 2017, the UIBE established the Institute of Regional and Country-Specific Studies, which was committed to integrating talents training and academic research with national development to promote disciplinary progress and build a high-end think tank. The Tunisia Studies Center became one of the 14 research centers under the institute.

The main research force of the center is composed of the faculty of the Department of Arabic and some teachers from the Department of French of the UIBE, including five professors, two associate professors and three lecturers. The center has invited scholars from the Carthage University Tunis and other universities to join the research team. In accordance with the overall arrangement and design by the Ministry of Education and the UIBE for regional and country-specific studies, it focuses its efforts on the studies of Tunisia and other countries in North Africa sharing similar history, culture and national situation with Tunisia.

As a think tank affiliated with a university, the center shoulders the responsibility of talent training. It is striving to mentor talents of global governance for the "Belt and Road" construction. By virtue of its majors of foreign languages, the center is working to integrate project research and international cooperation with talents training. The center gives full play to its synergic function, and by providing opportunities for students to study abroad, take short-term overseas visits, participate in project research and work as volunteers in foreign affairs, significantly improves students' language skills, academic research capabilities and comprehensive qualities, thus providing support for talent mentoring and foster high-level, inter-disciplinary and innovative foreign language talents for China-Tunisia cooperation. The center is also working hard to build a high-level academic group proficient in Arabic, English or French and capable of studying international issues. Through the establishment of the project team, young teachers, postgraduate students and doctoral students are absorbed into the team, thus providing opportunities for young researchers interested in studies of Tunisia and North Africa at large.

Starting with fundamental research, the center is enhancing its studies on Tunisia and gradually advancing its research on the North African region. The research area covers fundamental studies of Tunisian politics, economy, culture and diplomacy, historical studies of China-Tunisia relations, detailed issues of China-Tunisia cooperation, and regional research in North Africa. With the project-driven working mode, the center aims to break boundaries between different disciplines and build an open platform. Since its establishment, the center has undertaken two targeted projects of the International Department of the Ministry of Education, received approval of one scarce heritage project of the National Social Science Fund of China, completed one project sponsored by the

National Social Science Fund of China, and submitted more than 10 development reports to the information exchange platform for regional and country-specific studies. The researchers of the center have been successively invited to high-level international academic conferences including the round table of the China-Arab States Cooperation Forum hosted by the Ministry of Foreign Affairs; the China-Arab Youth Ambassadors Forum jointly hosted by the China-Arab Friendship Association, the Arab-China Friendship Association, and the League of Arab States; the Chinese African Forum for Higher Education hosted by the American University in Cairo, Egypt; and the Conference of Asian Arabists hosted by the Center for Research & Intercommunication Knowledge. The researchers of the center have undertaken the task of training cadres of African and Arabian countries assigned by China Foreign Languages Publishing Administration and other units, thus bolstering friendship between China and African countries as well as between China and Arabian countries. The center also puts a high value to its voice on international mainstream media. Huang Hui, director of the center, has given multiple interviews to mainstream media in African and Arabian countries including Tunisia, Algeria and the United Arab Emirates, as well as CGTN Arabic. She has also been invited to "Financial China" of CGTN Arabic.

In terms of international exchanges, the center has taken the advantage of the "China-Africa Universities 20+20 Cooperation Plan" to establish contact with the Carthage University Tunis and, starting from that point, has launched a series of activities of international academic exchanges. At the end of 2016, an academic team led by Huang Hui visited the Carthage University Tunis. After that, the center facilitated the signing of a sub-agreement on education cooperation between the School of Advanced Languages at the Carthage University Tunis and the School of Foreign Languages at the UIBE under the framework agreement of cooperation between the two universities. The two sides agreed to send teachers to each other's institutions to give lectures and carry out joint research. Since 2017, the center has organized three visits of academic delegations to Tunisia, received three Tunisian academic delegations, sent nearly 20 students to

Tunisia, and received eight Tunisian students. In 2017, the center took the lead and held the first China-Tunisia Joint Academic Symposium on Innovation and Entrepreneurship with the Carthage University Tunis. Since then, the center has held a session of the conference every year for three consecutive years, and has made great efforts to institutionalize the conference to build a high-end platform for academic exchanges between China and Tunisia.

In the future, the center will make continuous efforts to promote international cooperation and exchanges in scientific research and talent mentoring, and gradually develop itself into a well-known platform of Tunisian studies or even North African studies by bringing in talents and enhancing contact with domestic and foreign think tanks. On the basis of that, the center will submit policy advisory reports to related government departments, play an active role in China-Tunisia cooperation, and improve its capabilities of serving the government decision-making.

I. Contact Information

WeChat Official Account: gh_5c7762493df4

Contact person: Huang Hui; Email: huanghui@uibe.edu.cn

Correspondence Address: P. O. Box 127, University of International Business and Economics (100029), P. R. China.

Center for Tanzanian Studies, Communication University of China

I. Introduction

In July 2017, the Ministry of Education approved the establishment of a Center for Tanzanian Studies at the Communication University of China (CUC) as a Regional and Country-Specific Studies Center Registered with the Ministry of Education, and the Secretariat of the Regional and Country-Specific Studies Office issued the letter of approval. Afterwards, upon the approval of the Scientific Research Office of the CUC, the center was set up in the School of International Studies (SIS) and jointly supervised by the Secretariat of the Regional and Country-

Specific Studies Office and the SIS of the CUC. At the end of 2019, the CUC started the identification of research institutions and the center was recognized as one of the Other High-Level Scientific Research Institutions, and was put under the management of the SIS, with Ao Manyun as the director.

Based on the letter of approval from the Secretariat of the Regional and Country-Specific Studies Office, the center gives full play to the advantages of the CUC in disciplines, talents and technologies, combines the commission of the Ministry of Education with the operation of the CUC to achieve win-win cooperation.

The center practices a system of overall responsibility by the director. The director is appointed by the Scientific Research Office of the CUC, and reported to the Secretariat of the Regional and Country-Specific Studies Office. There are four members in the center, along with two part-time researchers and two foreign academic consultants.

Ao Manyun, director of the center, received a master's degree in Swahili in 2011, which was the first year such a degree had been granted. She is now pursuing a doctorate degree in Swahili in the University of Dar es Salaam in Tanzania, which will also be the first year for such a degree. She is also the only Chinese pursuing this degree. In recent years, the center has undertaken the tasks of translation of *Xi Jinping: The Governance of China (Volume I and Volume II)* into Swahili and subsequent proofreading.

In 2019, 12 students of Swahili graduated from the CUC. One of them was recruited by the Ministry of Foreign Affairs, one went to teach in the Information Engineering University, two found jobs in the State Security Bureau of Beijing, five pursued postgraduate studies at home or abroad, and three became self-employed. Currently, the CUC has 20 students of Grade 2019 majoring in Swahili.

In the future, the center will, based on political, economic, cultural, educational and other needs of China exposed during contact with African countries, carry out regional and country-specific studies on Tanzania and East Africa at large and become a think-tank type of research center. The specific goals are as follows:

providing consultancy services related to issues about target countries (regions); forming partnerships with think tanks and research institutions of target countries (regions); integrating industries with universities and research institutes to help Chinese enterprises go global and African enterprises settle in China; training talents of regional and country-specific studies (including the building of the curriculum and textbook system, education of undergraduates, selection of students to study abroad, and education of foreign students in China); irregularly organizing academic activities and people-to-people exchanges between China and Tanzania; and providing intellectual support for the establishment of the China-Tanzania cultural exchange mechanism.

II. Contact Information

Contact Person: Ao Manyun; Email: 961061988@qq.com

Correspondence Address: School of International Studies, Communication University of China, No. 1 Dingfuzhuang East Street, Chaoyang District, Beijing (100024), P. R. China.

Center for African Development Studies of College of International Development and Global Agriculture at China Agricultural University

I. Introduction

China Agricultural University (CAU) has been paying attention to African development since 2017, and has conducted fieldwork and research in various fields from different perspectives, including comparative studies on poverty and poverty reduction strategies of China and Africa, comparative studies on Chinese and African agriculture, comparative studies on Chinese and Japanese assistance to Tanzania, and studies on the roles of China and Brazil in African agricultural development. CAU has shifted its main efforts in the past three decades from "introducing foreign achievements into China" to "publicizing Chinese achievements abroad" in studies of international development and cooperation as well as talent training, particularly in studies of China-Africa agricultural cooperation and poverty reduction in the past decade. At the end of 2017, CAU and the Northwest A&F University jointly founded China Institute for South-South Cooperation in Agriculture. In 2018, the Center for African Studies was established. In December 2019, CAU established the College of International Development and Global Agriculture by integrating forces of China-Africa agricultural collaboration and research on the basis of the building of the think tank. Since then, studies of African development and talent cultivation have become the key to the development of New Agricultural Arts of the university.

The development goals of the center are as follows: conducting literature collection and field studies in the fields of China-Africa agricultural cooperation and African development, building an international platform based on the studies to promote high-level dialogues on policies and research in the two fields to generate new knowledge, formulating schemes of cultivating talents in the two fields, setting up a system of talent exchanges and cultivation between China and African countries, and giving demonstrations of African development and sharing China's development experience through field interactions.

The center altogether has 13 staff members, including eight professors and five associate professors. All the staff have doctoral degrees and overseas study or work experience. They are highly experienced in research and teaching of international development. In the following five years, as many as 15 high-level talents will be introduced to participate in the research in this field.

The center combines research, teaching and practice effectively from a perspective of development-oriented research. It focuses its research on China's role in the development of Africa from a perspective of development-oriented research. The research covers China's assistance to other countries, China's governmental and private investment in Africa, migration between China and Africa, and so on. In disciplinary construction, it will carry out studies on African development based on the discipline of international development, conduct comparative analysis of Africa from the views of China and western countries, and analyze the transformation of African politics, economy and society from a global view as well as issues of China-Africa cooperation. In empirical research, it pays great attention to the building of the data base. It works to obtain first-hand data of field investigations through participation on the basis of long-term and in-depth practice of Chinese and African agriculture and poverty reduction. In the construction of the talent system, it highlights fostering of novel-type talents for China-Africa cooperation and African development, and in particular, the improvement of the talents' capacity in integration of theories and practical skills.

By far, the research team has undertaken eight projects sponsored by first class research funds from home and abroad, including key projects and general projects of the National Social Science Fund of China; has won six awards at national and provincial levels; and has gained support of more than 30 research projects funded by the Ministry of Commerce, the Ministry of Foreign Affairs, the Ministry of Agriculture, China Development Bank, as well as international development organizations including the Bill & Melinda Gates Foundation, the Department for International Development of the UK, the United Nations Development Programme, and the Food and Agriculture Organization. The research team has published over 150 high-quality papers on top journals and key academic journals worldwide and 16 monographs. Besides, it has set up the first domestic system of fostering undergraduate students oriented towards international development, the first domestic system of mentoring graduate students oriented towards international development, and the first domestic system of fostering overseas students oriented towards international development. It has established the Township-Level Learning Center for Poverty Reduction in Tanzania, which is the first comprehensive overseas practice base integrating teaching, research and practice in foreign countries; set up China-Tanzania Joint Research Center; founded the first research and teaching institution in China with an international development organization as the practice base; and initiated the first China International Development Research Network (CIDRN), which raised attention in the industry around the globe.

Based on the disciplinary system of the College of Humanities and

Development Studies of CAU, the team has fostered nearly 10 Chinese doctors and postgraduates. They have completed their dissertations and theses about Tanzania, offering suggestions on China-Tanzania cooperation and industrial development of Tanzania. Additionally, more than 300 overseas students have graduated with master's or doctoral degrees, 95% of whom were African students.

The research team has established wide exchange and cooperation relations with governments, research institutions and universities of both developed and developing countries, among them are the Institute of Development Studies (IDS) at the University of Essex in the UK, the London School of Economics and Political Science (LSE), the Economic and Social Research Foundation (ESRF) and Sokoine University of Agriculture in Tanzania. In addition, it has conducted extensive cooperation with international organizations including the World Bank, the Bill & Melinda Gates Foundation, and the United Nations Development Programme.

II. Contact Information

Website: http://cissca.cau.edu.cn/

WeChat Official Account: CIDGA

Contact Person: Lu Jixia; Email: lujx@cau.edu.cn

Correspondence Address: College of Humanities and Development Studies, China Agricultural University, No. 2 Yuanmingyuan West Road, Haidian District, Bejing (100193), P. R. China.

Section of African Historical Studies, Institute of World History, Chinese Academy of Social Sciences

I. Introduction

In the spirit of the congratulatory letters sent by President Xi Jinping to the Chinese Academy of History and the Chinese Academy of African Studies, the Section of African Historical Studies in the Institute of World History at the Chinese Academy of Social Sciences (CASS) was officially established in early

December2019. At present, there are three researchers in the section, including two researchers and one associate researcher, all of them have doctoral degrees.

The section was established on the basis of the discipline of African historical studies set up by the Institute of World History at the CASS. The institute has long boasted strong research strength and academic influence in China in the field of African historical studies. Professor Peng Kunyuan is one of the major experts who planned the three-volume *Africa* (the volumes of Ancient, Modern and Contemporary Africa) published in 1995. He compiled the volume of Contemporary History together with Professor Lu Tingen of Peking University. Under the promotion of the Institute of World History and the approval of the Ministry of Civil Affairs, the Chinese Studies of African Historical Studies (CSAHS) was officially founded in 1980. The CSAHS has played an important role in leading the research, uniting research fellows, serving the society, providing advisory for the government and fostering talents. It mobilized research force nationwide to overcome difficulties in scientific research, and finished the above three-volume *Africa.* Bi Jiankang, director of the section, concurrently serves as the legal representative and secretary-general of the CSAHS.

The section mainly conducts studies on the history of the African region, the history of individual African countries and the history of Africa with a special theme. Its research focuses are the history of Southern Africa and that of North Africa. The discipline of African historical studies of the Institute of World History was approved as a Special Discipline by the CASS in 2010 and was listed into the Summit Program of the CASS as a special discipline in 2017. The discipline members have actively conducted academic exchanges with overseas counterparts, held multiple national academic conferences, undertaken and completed multiple projects sponsored by the National Social Science Fund of China, and published influential research results.

The main projects undertaken and completed by the researchers of the section include "Historical Investigation of the Relationship Between Apartheid System and Capitalist Economy in South Africa" (a project of the National Social Science

Fund of China led by Liu Lan); "Postwar Policy of the UK in British Sub-Saharan Africa" (a youth project of the National Social Science Fund of China led by Hang Cong); an Asian-African-Latin American sub-project of "Special Study on Social Changes and Social Stability in Foreign Countries Since Modern Times", (a key innovation project of the Chinese Academy of Social Sciences, with Bi Jiankang as the sub-project leader and Hang Cong as a project team member); "Observation of State, Religion and Development of Middle East Countries Through Iranian Issues" (a fundamental scholar's program of the Chinese Academy of Social Sciences led by Bi Jiankang); "Comparative Study on Democracy in the Modernization Process of the Middle East" (a youth project of the National Social Science Fund of China, with Bi Jiankang as the project leader and Liu Lan as a project team member); and "Study of Postwar Anglo-American Neo-Colonialism" (with Zhang Shunhong as the research group leader and Bi Jiankang as a research group member).

II. Contact Information

Contact Person: Hang Cong; Tel: +86-10-87421031; Email: hangcong@cass.org.cn

Correspondence Address: Room 315, Building 3, No. 1 National Stadium North Road, Chaoyang District, Beijing (100101), P. R. China.

Institute of African & Latin American Studies, Institute for International Strategic Studies, Party School of Central Committee of CPC (National Academy of Governance)

I. Introduction

The Institute for International Strategic Studies at the Party School of the Central Committee of CPC (National Academy of Governance) is mainly engaged in studies on major theoretical and strategic issues of Chinese diplomacy and national security. The institute attaches great importance to African studies and set up the Department of African Studies, a platform for academic research, in 2102, and on the basis of that, established a physical entity, the Institute of African & Latin American Studies, in 2019. The Institute for International Strategic Studies undertook the China-Africa Joint Research and Exchange Program of the Ministry of Foreign Affairs in 2012 and became a partner of the "China-Africa Think Tanks 10+10 Partnership Plan" of the FOCAC in 2013. It is also engaged in long-term academic cooperation with the Institute of Peace and Security Studies (IPSS) at Addis Ababa University in Ethiopia.

The Department of African Studies mainly studies China's strategies and policies towards Africa, national governance, China's assistance to other countries, the African Union and African integration, major countries' policies towards Africa etc.

It focuses on major fundamental, strategic and future-oriented issues on China-Africa relations and African development, and fully embodies theoretical depth, strategic height and global vision of the Party School of the Central Committee of CPC (National Academy of Governance). Through academic research, policy advisory, and domestic and foreign academic exchanges, it is bound to become a think tank of African studies with domestic influence and international reputation.

The department has undertaken five projects sponsored by the National Social Science Fund of China, and over 20 provincial and ministerial level projects including those funded by the Party School of the Central Committee of CPC (National Academy of Governance), the Ministry of Foreign Affairs, the International Department of the Central Committee of CPC, the Ministry of Commerce, the Ministry of Education, and the State Council Information Office. It has completed multiple key projects entrusted by the central government. It has published six books and one translated book of African studies including *China-Africa Relations and China's Responsibilities as a Major Country, The Road to Renaissance: Studies on the African Union and African Integration, China-Africa Development Cooperation: Studies on the Theories, Strategies and Policies*. It has published over a hundred academic papers on well-known domestic and foreign journals like *World Economics and Politics, Foreign Affairs Review, Quarterly*

Journal of International Politics, West Asia and Africa, Journal of Contemporary Asia-Pacific Studies and *Review of International Studies* (Cambridge University Press). It has also submitted multiple research and consultancy reports to the central government and related government departments.

The department has long been engaged in the training of party and government cadres of African countries organized by the Party School of the Central Committee of CPC (National Academy of Governance) and has established long-term cooperation with the Federal Meles Zenawi Leadership Academy of Ethiopia and the National School of Administration of Algeria. In recent years, teachers of the Institute for International Strategic Studies have visited over 20 countries including Ethiopia, Kenya, South Africa, Sudan, South Sudan, Angola, Sierra Leone and Nigeria for field research and academic seminars. Meanwhile, the institute has received multiple scholars and government officials from African countries as well as European and American scholars studying African issues.

II. Contact Information

Contact Person: Luo Jianpo; Tel: +86-10-62805137; Email: luojb@ccps.gov.cn

Correspondence Address: Institute for International Strategic Studies, Party School of Central Committee of CPC (National Academy of Governance), No. 100 Dayouzhuang, Haidian District, Beijing (100091), P. R. China.

East Africa (Indonesia) Research Center of Chongqing Normal University

I. Introduction

The East Africa (Indonesia) Research Center of Chongqing Normal University, established in November 2012, is a university-level key scientific research platform based on the College of Foreign Languages and Literatures and run by the International College of Chinese Language and Culture. In June 2017, the center was recognized as a Regional and Country-Specific Studies Center Registered with the Ministry of Education.

It mainly studies culture, language, education and history of East Africa as well as China-Africa cooperation in education.

The center has 18 researchers, including 15 from the College of Foreign Languages, two from the College of History and Social Science, and one from the College of Liberal Arts. Among them there are five professors, 11 associate professors and 10 doctors. Professor Zeng Xuemei is the director of the center.

Since its establishment, the center has made important achievements in African studies, including *Studies of Rwandan Language, Education and Social Development*, *Rwanda & English & Chinese Dictionary*, and *Handbook of Education in Rwanda.*

II. Contact Information

Contact Person: Zeng Xuemei; Tel: +86-23-65362742; Email: 2534194838@qq.com

Correspondence Address: College of Foreign Languages and Literatures, Chongqing Normal University (401331), P. R. China.

Benin Research Center, Chongqing Jiaotong University

I. Introduction

The Benin Research Center of Chongqing Jiaotong University, established in June 2017, is a Regional and Country-Specific Studies Center Registered with the Ministry of Education.

With "improving the capability of consultancy for decision-making" at its core, the center conducts comprehensive studies on politics, economy, culture and society of Benin and surrounding countries as well as political, social, economic and cultural influence brought by China's Africa-assistance projects. It is committed to promoting the development of research on university transportation culture, promulgation of national and city images, tourism economy, engineering Chinese and engineering culture, and teaching Chinese to speakers of other languages (TCSOL). It also aims to further enhance cooperation with the Chinese

Embassy in Benin, the Chinese Cultural Center in Benin and Chinese-invested enterprises in Benin, and set up the dynamic risk warning mechanism for Benin and surrounding countries.

The center gives full play to the platform advantage of the Confucius Institute co-founded by Chongqing Jiaotong University and the University of Abomey-Calavi in Benin, the theoretical advantage of research on the influence of China's Africa-assistance projects, the historical advantage of China's assistance to Africa, and the discipline advantage of transportation projects and culture. By integrating resources, the center carries out various studies and plays an active role in the studies of hot issues about Benin and West Africa at large.

The center has independent premises, complete facilities and a specialized academic website. Its academic committee consists of experts from home and abroad. Among them are foreign experts including professor Joël Bellassen from France and professor Segbo Julien A. Gaetan from Benin, and over 10 domestic experts including professor Wang Hui from Zhejiang Normal University, and professor Zhang Shangyi, deputy president of Chongqing Jiaotong University.

The center actively organizes academic seminars, conducts in-depth research, and combines fundamental research with application studies. It has completed *Handbook of Education in Benin*, and two scientific research projects of the Ministry of Education, namely, "Development and Cooperation of High-tech Industries in Africa and China's Cooperation Strategy—A Case Study of Benin", and "Research Report on the Political and Party System of Benin—History, Present Situation and Operation". In addition, it has initiated work related to the fostering of research projects on Benin to encourage more experts and scholars to join them.

The center advances the recruitment of postgraduate students in the University of Abomey-Calavi and other universities or institutions qualified for enrolling postgraduate students to study China-Benin relations. It works hard to develop undergraduate courses of TCSOL, increase the enrollment of students from Benin, and adjust the scholarship policy moderately to favor students from Benin. It is committed to the development of "2+2" and "1+3" projects in the School of Civil Engineering, the College of Traffic & Transportation, the School of Shipping and Naval Architecture, and the School of Humanities. It is working to increase the total number of students from Benin, increase the enrollment of the "Overseas Engineer" project in Benin, and steadily promote the projects of Chinese language training and Chinese cultural experience at multiple levels in various ways in Benin and West Africa at large.

While analyzing hot issues about Benin and West Africa at large, the center has also brought up its development plan for the future, namely, gathering strength, specifying four key directions and establishing four institutes including the Institute for the Development of Benin and West Africa at Large, the Institute for China-Benin People-to-People Exchanges, the Institute for Transportation Development in Benin and West Africa at Large, and the Institute for the Development of Teaching Chinese to Students of Other Languages in Benin and West Africa at Large. The Institute for the Development of Benin and West Africa at Large will center around Benin and other West African countries to carry out research on local politics, economy, culture and relative areas. The Institute for China-Benin People-to-People Exchanges will mainly conduct studies on people-to-people exchanges between China and Benin, including Beninese people's understanding of, imagination about, and identification with China, social network and interaction among Chinese-speaking people in Benin, Beninese people's impressions and attitudes about China after they return home from China, the potential of Beninese tourism economy, the popularity and challenges of Chinese products in Benin, and China's national image in Benin. By virtue of the disciplinary feature of Chongqing Jiaotong University, especially its transportation studies, the Institute for Transportation Development in Benin and West Africa at Large will focus on studies of transportation development in Benin and West Africa at large. The Institute for the Development of Teaching Chinese to Students of Other Languages in Benin and West Africa at Large will, on one hand, fully utilize its advantages and integrate resources to train practical talents of "Chinese + vocational expertise", on the other hand, enhance its research on Chinese language education and teaching, including the mechanism and strategies of China-Benin educational exchanges related to Chinese language education, Benin's educational system and the building of national consciousness, the forming of the influence of Chinese educational concept and system in Benin, the acceptance and development of Chinese traditional sports in Benin, and the development of Chinese language education in Benin and West Africa at large.

II. Contact Information

Website: http://bnyjzx.cqjtu.edu.cn/

Contact Person: Tang Juan; Email: 645451585@qq.com

Correspondence Address: No. 66 Xuefu Avenue, Nan'an District, Chongqing (400074), P. R. China.

Africa Research Center of the Belt and Road Research Institute, Xiamen University

I. Introduction

The Africa Research Center (ARC) of the Belt and Road Research Institute, Xiamen University was established in 2018, in correspondence with the University's motto of "Pursue Excellence; Strive for Perfection". The center aims to promote and sustain original and cutting-edge research on Africa, Africans, and people of African descent around the world within an open, multidisciplinary framework. As a multidisciplinary research unit, the ARC strives to build bridges and foster continuous dialogues between physics-nature and humanities-social sciences on contemporary issues in the African research agenda, and to improve the understanding of Africa and Africans in the Chinese academic community, so as to strengthen China-Africa cooperation, build the "Belt and Road Initiative", and achieve the common development of China and Africa in the future.

Professor Augustin Holl, Director of the ARC, is a distinguished professor at Xiamen University, an invited professor at the University of Dakar, a chair professor at the University of Yaoundé I, a research fellow at the American Field Museum of Natural History, a research fellow at African Languages and Traditional Literature Research Center, and the chairman of the International Scientific Committee of UNESCO General History of Africa (Volumes IX-XI). His research interests include the origins of food production, the origins of social complexity in West Africa and the Levant, rock painting archaeology, and ancient tomb archaeology. He has conducted archaeological fieldwork in Negev of Israel, northern Cameroon, northwestern Burkina Faso, and south-central Senegal, and is currently directing a scientific research project on shell middens in the Saloum Delta in the coastal area of Senegal. He has published 14 books, edited or co-edited three books, and numerous articles in peer-reviewed journals and books, with a current research focusiug on global comparative archaeology.

While still in the process of development, the ARC will promote multidisciplinary research and teaching on Africa and people of African descent worldwide. It plans to recruit researchers with backgrounds in environmental science, traditional Chinese medicine, economics, sociology, and other disciplines as its core team, and is expecting to form a research team in the fall semester of 2021.

The ARC will first discuss cooperation with the University of Ghana in Ghana, Kiyabii University in Kenya, and the Federal University of Minas Gerais in Brazil. The new Museum of Black Civilizations in Dakar, Senegal, which was built with the assistance of the Chinese government, has been completed, and the archaeological project on shell middens in the Saloum Delta, proposed in July 2018 with the participation of eight undergraduate students from Xiamen University, will be launched as soon as possible through the signing of a memorandum of understanding. The center will organize a series of scientific research and exchange activities, such as symposiums, international conferences, and lectures by distinguished scholars and personages from home and abroad.

The ARC, part of the Belt and Road Research Institute, Xiamen University, is moving ahead. This growing program will add diversity and richness to the teaching and research building of Xiamen University. It will take a series of new initiatives to make the center one of the leading institutions for the study of Africa and its diaspora in the next decade, and it is hoped that the ARC will contribute to the deepening of academic exchanges and cooperation among higher education institutions in China, Africa, and the black world at large.

II. Contact Information

Contact Person: Augustin F. C. Holl; Email: gaochang@xmu.edu.cn

Han Xiuli (vice director of the center); Email: hanxiu777@xmu.edu.cn

Correspondence Address: School of Sociology and Anthropology, Xiamen University, No. 422 Siming South Road, Siming District, Xiamen City, Fujian Province, P. R. China (361005), P. R. China.

West Asian & East African Studies Center of the National Ethnic Affairs Commission

I. Introduction

The West Asian & East African Studies Center of the National Ethnic Affairs Commission of the People's Republic of China (NEAC) was approved in December 2018 and founded in the Northwest Minzu University on the basis of its School of Foreign Languages. It plans to carry out research in the fields of economy and trade, energy security, international relations and social issues in 17 countries including Lebanon, Jordan, Syria, Palestine, Israel, Saudi Arabia, Kuwait, Qatar, Bahrain, Iraq, Yemen, Oman and the United Arab Emirates of West Asia as well as Somalia, Djibouti, Ethiopia and Eritrea of East Africa.

Based on the advantages of foreign language disciplines and incorporating the outstanding resources of politics, economics, humanities and other disciplines, the center conducts research in such fields as politics, economy, energy, history, law and humanities in relevant regions and countries. By doing so, it promotes the intensive development of academic research, strengthens the linkage mechanism of interdisciplinary research and multi-level cooperation in introducing intelligence, broadens research channels, and fosters cross-disciplinary and interdisciplinary national and regional research talents. It aims to develop into a research institute that provides scientific advisory and services for high-quality educational development and talent training of the university as well as local economic prosperity, and gradually become one of the regional and national research centers of the NEAC providing quality services for social prosperity, economic development and humanistic harmony in the western region.

The center conducts fundamental research in the following five fields: economy and trade (including marine resources, port construction and fishery export), energy security (cooperation in oil and natural gas; development and utilization of new energy, green energy and renewable energy), translation studies (translation of Chinese and foreign cultural classics), social culture (educational environment, legal system, folk culture, social thoughts, international relations and regional hot issues) and language communication (language ecology, dialects, language and communication, etc.). In the future, it plans to conduct domestic fundamental research and strengthens cooperation with relevant foreign academic institutes and think tanks to carry out cutting-edge research in related academic fields and provide quality advisory services.

The center has an academic committee for the work related to academic research and a general office for daily administration. The center currently has eight full-time researchers and 12 part-time researchers.

The center has published a significant research achievement *Research on Social Reformers of Egypt in the 19th Century* (China Social Sciences Press, January 2019) and a number of academic papers, which are well accepted by the academic community. In addition, its researchers participated in regional and national academic seminars held by domestic universities such as Sun Yat-Sen University, Yunnan Minzu University, and Dalian Minzu University, gradually bringing the center onto the domestic stage. Toward the end of 2020, the center began to offer optional courses of regional and national research for undergraduates and postgraduates to guide them into the field of regional and national cross-disciplinary research on the basis of the foreign language in the context of the New Liberal Arts so as to meet the needs of the national strategy and economic construction.

II. Contact Information

Contact Person: Ma Hebin; Tel: +86-13609345027; Email: mwxydfcentre2018@126.com-

Correspondence Address: School of Foreign Languages, Northwest Minzu University, Chengguan District, Lanzhou City, Gansu Province (730124), P. R. China.

Research Center for Sudan & South Sudan, Northwest Normal University

I. Introduction

Gansu Province established contact with Sudan quite early. In 1995, China National Petroleum Corporation set up in Sudan its first overseas institution, Khartoum Refinery Company Limited, which was built and jointly managed by Lanzhou Petrochemical Company. In the past twenty years, Khartoum Refinery Company Limited has played a pivotal role in the national economy of Sudan. In 2005, the Northwest Normal University sent volunteer Chinese teachers to work in the Chinese Department of the University of Khartoum. In 2009, the two universities signed a cooperation agreement and jointly set up a Confucius Institute at the University of Khartoum, which accommodates a China-Sudan Language and Culture Research Center, to comprehensively promote teaching of Chinese in Sudan and advance cultural exchanges between the two countries. In October 2019, the Northwest Normal University established the National and Regional Research Institute, which houses four research centers including the Research Center for Sudan & South Sudan.

The center was established in response to the needs of educational opening up

in the new era. It integrates resources of teaching Chinese to speakers of other languages (TCSOL), history, Chinese, media, tourism, law and other disciplines and gives full play to the platform and resource advantages of the Confucius Institute at the University of Khartoum. Taking into consideration the need of the university in internationalized development, the center focuses its research on politics, economy, education, culture, ethnic groups and other issues of Sudan to provide advisory services for government decision-making and think tank support for sustainable development of the Confucius Institute, which is bound to help deepen China-Africa friendship and promote people-to-people exchanges. The key area of research in the past three years mainly involves the policies of the transitional government of Sudan towards China, the relations between Sudan and South Sudan, cooperative development of tourism and cultural resources of Sudan, Sudan-China archaeological cooperation, ancient civilizations of Sudan, China-Sudan and China-South Sudan cultural cooperation, China-Sudan and China-South Sudan educational cooperation, disputes over water rights in the Nile River reaches, the political ecology of the countries along the Nile River, investment risks of Chinese-funded enterprises in Sudan and South Sudan, sustainable development of Confucius Institutes in Sudan, China-Sudan cooperation in wasteland treatment, China-Sudan cooperation in vocational education, and Chinese translation of Sudanese common laws.

The center is affiliated to the National and Regional Research Institute of the Northwest Normal University and is run by the College of International Cultural Exchanges. Still in its infancy, the center has a total of four full-time and part-time researchers and hires foreign researchers from Sudan, the United Arab Emirates and other countries. The director of the center is Professor Tian He, deputy dean of the College of International Cultural Exchanges and former Chinese dean of the Confucius Institute at the University of Khartoum.

In recent years, the Northwest Normal University has successively fostered more than 30 doctors in physics, mathematics and chemistry and nearly 40 masters of TCSOL for Sudan. They have become the backbone of China-Sudan cultural exchanges and Chinese teaching in Sudan as well as native scholars that can be relied on in this center. In August 2020, the center recruited three Sudanese doctors of TCSOL with the "Cooperative Scholarship of the Confucius Institute at the Northwest Normal University" to focus on Chinese education to international students in Sudan and China-Sudan cultural exchanges.

Looking forward to the future, the center plans to form a stable research team; set up a center website to regularly release the latest information on culture, education and politics of Sudan and South Sudan, which is expected to become the most important website for Chinese people to understand the region; publish influential research achievements and publish annual research reports of Sudan and South Sudan; and promote the implementation of the "Chinese plus vocational education" project in Sudan and strengthen the study of vocational education in Sudan and South Sudan to serve the overall needs of China's diplomacy and education.

II. Contact Information

Contact Person: Tian He; Tel: +86-931-7971812; Email: tianhe999@126.com

Correspondence Address: P. O. Box 21, College of International Cultural Exchanges, Northwest Normal University, No. 967 Anning East Road, Lanzhou City, Gansu Province (730070), P. R. China.

Institute for African Studies, Guangdong University of Foreign Studies

I. Introduction

The Institute for African Studies (IAS) at Guangdong University of Foreign Studies was inaugurated by former state councilor, Mr. Dai Bingguo, on November 22, 2016. Over the past three years since its establishment, the IAS has adhered to its orientation of practical studies, centered around addressing problems and completing tasks, persisted in the "three combinations", namely, combining its research with the general direction of the Central Committee's work toward Africa, Guangdong Province's central work toward Africa, and the needs of Guangdong's enterprises to enter African market, and preliminarily established an approach of African practical studies, which is expected to serve as an important supplement for China's research on Africa.

The main functions of the IAS are as follows: (1) carrying out fundamental theoretical research on economic, political, cultural and diplomatic issues of Africa as a whole and its individual countries; (2) cooperating withrelevant national authorities (such as the Ministry of Foreign Affairs, the National Development and Reform Commission, the Ministry of Commerce, and Guangdong Provincial Government) to provide research reports and policy advisory on hot issues; (3) providing services to local governments on investment and economic cooperation in Africa (establishment of economic cooperation and investment projects by local governments in Africa) including policy advisory and planning of economic parks; (4) providing consultancy services on investment policies, investment planning and other aspects for commercial enterprises intended to invest in Africa; (5) attending and hosting conferences and forums on African studies, investment in Africa and African affairs, inviting African guests to China to give lectures, and organizing domestic experts to give lectures in Africa; and (6) fostering talents for African countries in economic management, diplomacy and other fields, and training vocational and technical personnel for African countries in light of their specific needs.

Under the IAS are the Research Center on Investment and Trade in Africa, the Global Marketing and Research Center for Chinese Cultural Brands, the East Africa Studies Center, the "Belt and Road" Business Talents Collaborative Training Center, and the "Belt and Road" Chinese Medicine Talents Collaborative Training Center. There are now 35 full-time and part-time researchers in the IAS. It has also formed innovation teams of African regional and country-specific studies. The institute is now one of the Regional and Country-Specific Studies Centers Registered with the Ministry of Education and has advanced physical construction in accordance with the requirements of the Ministry of Education.

Over the past three years, the institute has undertaken 27 projects entrusted by national ministries and commissions, Guangdong Provincial Government, prefectural and municipal governments of Guangdong, and enterprises of Guangdong. Among them, "Research on the Integration of the 'Belt and Road' Initiative with the African Union", a project commissioned by the "Belt and Road" Think Tank Alliance of the International Department, Central Committee of CPC, was awarded the prize of excellent achievements. It has also undertaken two projects of China-Africa Joint Research on People-to-People Exchanges commissioned by the Ministry of Foreign Affairs. It has written 15 research reports. Five of them have received instructions and comments from heads of the CPC provincial committee and the provincial government, one of them was published on *People's Daily*, and two of them were adopted by the General Office of the CCCPC.

In 2018, the IAS initiated the "Belt and Road" African Studies Alliance along with African studies institutions, key enterprises and business associations at home and abroad. Now the alliance has 16 members from China, 16 members from Africa and two members from Europe. It will try to include one or two think tanks from each of 54 African countries in five years.

The IAS joins hands with Guangzhou University of Chinese Medicine and Guangdong Provincial Hospital of Chinese Medicine to foster talents of traditional Chinese medicine to help traditional Chinese medicine enter the African market. It also works together with the School of Business at Guangdong University of Foreign Studies and the Overseas Investment Union of the National Development and Reform Commission to set up African classes, achieving seamless integration of Chinese entrepreneurs with African businesses, promoting smooth trade transactions and capacity improvement of African countries, accelerating the transfer of China's vehicle maintenance technology to Africa, and promoting the export of China's second-hand vehicles and the establishment of the supply chain of auto parts.

The IAS has set up the Kenyan Research base in East Africa, the South African Research Base in Southern Africa and the Egyptian Research Base in North

Africa. In 2020, it will establish the Nigerian Research Base in West Africa, and meanwhile initiate the development of international cooperation between the Egyptian Research Base and the South African Research Base, with both sides inputting capital and researchers to conduct joint studies, share research fruits and jointly publish papers and books. Since its establishment, the IAS has visited Africa three times and established contact with government departments, Chinese embassies and consulates, Chinese business associations, industrial parks, research institutions and universities in Ethiopia, Nigeria, Ghana, Kenya, Uganda, South Africa and Egypt. Thus, it has obtained more resources on African studies. The IAS has established business cooperation with 11 consulates general of African countries in Guangzhou, thus setting up a smooth dialogue mechanism. In addition, it has built a business dialogue mechanism with nine African business associations in Guangzhou, which serves as a bridge and link for information exchanges, joint research and fruit sharing.

The IAS is committed to making itself a southern highland of China's applied research on Africa in five to eight years, contributing to the entry of Chinese enterprises into Africa and the improvement of China's influence in Africa.

II. Contact Information

Website: https://ias.gdufs.edu.cn/

WeChat Official Account: ias-gdufs

Contact Person: Liu Jisen; Email: 165596976@qq.com

Correspondence Address: Room 307, MBA Education Center, Guangdong University of Foreign Studies, No. 2 Baiyun Avenue, Guangzhou City, Guangdong Province, P. R. China.

Center for African Studies, School of Sociology & Anthropology, Sun Yat-sen University

I. Introduction

The Center for African Studies at the School of Sociology & Anthropology of Sun Yat-sen University was established in 2017. Relying on the profound discipline advantages of the School of Sociology & Anthropology, it has actively expanded its research to the African region. The center is headed by Professor Zhu Tiequan from the School of Sociology & Anthropology, with associate researcher Chen Liang as the executive director. It has formed a core research team with researchers from the School of Sociology & Anthropology and the School of Government, and the researchers conduct regular exchanges.

Focusing on the "Belt and Road" Initiative and strategic needs of building a community with a shared future for China and Africa, the center promotes disciplinary development through specific studies on Africa. In the context of the "Belt and Road" Initiative and the increasingly frequent non-governmental exchanges between China and Africa, it has carried out research in social sciences on such topics as immigration, business investment and cultural exchanges.

The scientific research activities of the center are focused on the two fields of archaeology and social anthropology. In archaeology, the advantages of archaeometry are applied to explore how ancient China-Africa connections were strengthened through the cross-ocean trade networks. In 2012 and 2017, the center conducted archaeological excavations on Manda Island of Lamu Archipelago in Kenya, and researchers discovered a large number of Chinese porcelains from different periods, two coins of Yongle Tongbao, four Chinese glazed beads, three suspected Chinese bone remains. In terms of social anthropology, the center has incorporated African studies into the framework of the building of the China-Africa community and the "Belt and Road" Initiative, and paid attention to development, commerce, people-to-people and cultural exchanges as well as mechanisms between China and Africa. Specific scientific research results include: (1) questionnaire surveys on African businessmen and overseas students in Guangzhou, which involves most of African countries; surveys on cross-border marriage between China and Africa; research on cross-border trade intermediaries; research on the establishment of network images of Africans; and research on informal governance of Africans in China; (2) cultural anthropology research on the nomads in Ethiopia's border areas since 2017; and (3) studies on the internal ethnic relations, cultural differences and understanding of enterprises investing in Ethiopia.

In June 2018, the center held the first "Conference of Ancient and Modern China-Africa Connections", an international academic symposium focusing on exploring the connections between China and Africa in archaeology, immigration, and companies in Africa. In December 2019, the center held a workshop of "Field Investigation Methods in African Anthropology Research" for the second "Conference of Ancient and Modern China-Africa Connections" to promote research on the methods of field investigations in Africa within the disciplines of anthropology, linguistics and others.

Since its establishment, the center has established sound academic partnerships with the Institute of Ethiopian Studies (IES) of Addis Ababa University, Semara University and other institutions.

II. Contact Information

Contact Person: Chen Liang; Email: chenliang9@mail.sysu.edu.cn

Correspondence Address: Martin Hall, No. 135 Xingang West Road, Guangzhou City, Guangdong Province (510275), P. R. China.

Center for African Studies, Wuhan University

I. Introduction

The Center for African Studies at Wuhan University is an academic institution focusing on African studies and was established in 2010 on the basis of the Department of French of the university. With the comprehensive university's multi-disciplinary and French-language advantages, the center integrates and mobilizes relevant resources of the university, and maintains a long-term comprehensive cooperative relationship with more than 40 universities and research institutions in France and Francophone countries of Africa, including the University of Paris, Clermont-Ferrand II University, Bordeaux Montaigne

University, Jean Moulin University Lyon 3, the University of La Rochelle, and the University of Lorraine in France; University Hassan-I in Morocco; the University of Cotonou in Benin; the University of Social Sciences and Management of Bamako in Mali; the University of Sfax in Tunisia; Cheikh Anta Diop University in Senegal; Alexandria University and Benha University in Egypt; Omar Bongo University in Gabon; and Capital University in Guinea. Since its establishment, the Center for African Studies has been actively forging cooperative relations with foreign institutions on African studies, learning from them, and co-training master's and doctoral candidates with relevant institutions to provide outstanding young talents of African studies for China. The center became a member of the Agence Universitaire de la Francophonie (AUF) in 2013 and a Regional and Country-Specific Studies Center Registered with the Ministry of Education in 2017.

The incumbent director of the center is Professor Wang Zhan, deputy dean of the School of Foreign Languages and Literatures of Wuhan University, head of the French Department, a social economist, and an expert of African studies. The center owns five full-time professors, three associate professors, two lecturers and dozens of master's and doctoral students, and embraces multiple hot-spot research fields such as African society and culture, languages and literature, and inter-cultural communication.

Since its establishment, the center has actively carried out the work of intellectual introduction. Over the past five years, the center invited 10 to 20 experts from France and Francophone countries of Africa every year to give lectures or conduct joint research. Among them are more than 100 visiting experts of African studies including Nobel Prize winner Jean-Marie Gustave Le Clézio; Academician Anna Cheng of the Institut de France; Inspector-General of Chinese Language Teaching Joël Bellassen of the French Ministry of Education; Vice President Bernadette Bricout of Paris Diderot University; President Brice Sinsin of the University of Cotonou in Benin; Vice Chancellor Ahmadou Aly Mbaye of Cheikh Anta Diop University in Senegal; Director Didier Nativel of the Centre for Social Science Studies on the African, American and Asian Worlds at the University of Paris; and Director Mehdi Ghouirgate of the Department of Arabic Studies at Bordeaux Montaigne University. Starting from the perspectives of politics, economy, history, international relations, geography, science and technology as well as cultures of Francophone countries, they have offered cutting-edge theories and knowledge to teachers and students of the French Department, as well as young scholars and master's and doctoral candidates who are interested in African studies. The lectures given by guest scholars have optimized the teaching content of the French major, enhanced the level of regional and country-specific studies of the center, and laid the foundation for the implementation of the "Belt and Road" Initiative in Africa and cultivation of interdisciplinary talents. The work of intellectual introduction has also promoted in-depth development of the internationalization of the French Department. The department has established partnerships with the Centre for Social Science Studies on the African, American and Asian Worlds at Paris Diderot University, the Africas in the World Laboratory at Bordeaux Montaigne University, the Francophone Research Base at the University of Clermont Auvergne, the Research Institute of the "Silk and Road" at University Hassan-I, the Economic Development Institute at Cheikh Anta Diop University. They have held programs of teachers' mutual visits and student exchanges, and jointly fostered nearly 20 doctoral students in history, geography, economics, sociology, literature and others. These students' dissertations "Risk Identification of Chinese Investment in Africa", "Research on Cultural Integration of Chinese Businessmen in Algeria", "Research on Chinese in situ Urbanization Based on the French Urbanization Model" and "Analysis on Yiwu Competition and Integration Factors Attracting African Businessmen" and others have passed defense in France and China.

In 2017, Wuhan University, based on the work of intellectual introduction, established a mechanism for higher education cooperation among China, France and Africa, and held the first forum in the same year. The second forum was held at Hassan-I University in Casablanca in 2018, and the third forum was held at Paris Diderot University in 2019. Presidents, scholars and doctoral students from more than 20 universities of Francophone countries and over 50 Chinese universities attended the forums. They discussed various topics on African policies, institutions, and religious culture, and also made prospects for the potential cooperation among the three parties.

In 2019, the Center for African Studies published two monographs of African studies, published 14 Africa-related papers and reviews, undertook nine research projects (including eight at the national level), and submitted four consultancy reports that were adopted by national ministries and commissions. The center invited six experts of African studies to give lectures and sent researchers to participate in a number of academic conferences at home and abroad. The academic influence of the center is continuing to strengthen.

II. Contact Information

WeChat Account: WHU Francophone Studies

Contact Person: Wang Zhan; Email: wangz13@aliyun.com

Correspondence Address: School of Foreign Languages and Literature of Wuhan University, Luojiashan, Wuchang District, Wuhan City, Hubei Province (430072), P. R. China.

China-Africa Institute for Business and Law, Xiangtan University

I. Introduction

The China-Africa Institute for Business and Law at Xiangtan University developed from the African Research Office of Xiangtan University established in September 1978 upon the instruction of the central government. The institute is the first academic institution of African studies established in China's universities after the reform and opening up. In 1998, it was transformed into the Research Institute of African Law. In 2005, it was expanded into the Research Center for African Law and Society. In June 2019, the institute was renamed the China-Africa Institute for Business and Law.

The institute, headed by Professor Hong Yonghong, currently has 28 full-time researchers, including 11 professors, eight associate professors, and nine lecturers, and 27 of them have obtained doctoral degrees. Among them, one expert enjoys the special government allowance of the State Council, one is in the list of the National Hundred, Thousand and Ten Thousand Talents Project, two have won the Baosteel Outstanding Teacher Awards, two are listed in the New Century Excellent Talents Support Program of the Ministry of Education, and 10 researchers have gained at least one year of experience as visiting scholars. They can teach in English and French fluently. In addition, the institute has also invited five part-time professors from major domestic African research institutions and four part-time professors from well-known universities in South Africa, Ethiopia and Uganda.

The institute boasts a solid platform foundation and a mature operating mechanism, and has formed the characteristic of coordinated promotion of educational cooperation, legal research and cultural exchanges. First, in terms of educational cooperation, in 2010, Xiangtan University was selected to participate in the "China-Africa Universities 20+20 Cooperation Plan" and has forged a partnership with Makerere University in Uganda, which ranks the first in East Africa. Second, in terms of legal research, in 2012, the China Law Society designated the institute as the "African Law Training Base in China", and in 2018, it became the permanent host unit of the "China-Africa Forum of Law School Deans". Third, in terms of cultural exchanges, in 2014, Makerere University and Xiangtan University jointly established a Confucius Institute. Its Chinese director was Professor Hong Yonghong, the director of the institute. The Confucius Institute provides a platform for the institute to carry out cultural exchanges between China and Africa.

The institute has yielded abundant research results with strong academic and social influence, and made fruitful achievements in talent fostering. The members of the institute have published more than 30 academic monographs and more than 150 papers in the field of African law. The institute published China's first academic monograph on African law *Introduction to African Law* in 2000 and launched China's first academic journal on African law *African Law Review* in 2015. It has obtained achievements in five areas, namely, African traditional Legal Culture, African human rights and diplomacy, African department law, African law of trade and investment, and China-Africa legal dispute resolution. Among them, works such as *History of Legal Development in Africa*, *Studies on Private International Law of the Republic of South Africa*, and *Studies of the Rwandan Criminal Court* have great influences in the academic community. Meanwhile, the institute vigorously promotes exchanges and practical cooperation between China and Africa by means of conferences and forums. It has successively hosted more than 30 large-scale China-Africa legal cooperation conferences and held more than 40 academic lectures on Chinese and African law. Members of the institute have been invited to participate in activities including the national "Forum on China-Africa Cooperation-Legal Forum" multiple times.

The institute boasts a complete and effective talent fostering system, with outstanding achievements in curricula, teaching materials and postgraduate education. The institute began to recruit master students on African law in 1999. "African Law" was included in the national textbook for the first time in 2003 as a special chapter. In response to the needs of students of different academic levels, the institute has compiled African law textbooks for undergraduate and postgraduate students. In 2010, it began to recruit doctoral candidates on African law, and in 2012 it began to recruit African students to study African law in China. Up till now, the institute has fostered more than 100 master's and doctoral graduates in Africa studies. In recent years, more than 10 graduate students from the institute have been sponsored by the state to study in Africa.

Taking scientific research projects and practical consultancy services as the starting point, the institute has undertaken more than 50 research projects to meet the needs of cooperation with Africa at the national and provincial level. Since 2005, the members of the institute have undertaken over 10 projects of the National Social Science Fund of China, over 20 provincial and ministerial-level projects, and over 10 projects commissioned by enterprises. The projects of the National Social Science Fund of China mainly include "Research on Restrictive Foreign Employment Laws in African Countries and the Responses of Chinese Enterprises", "Research on Dispute Settlement Mechanism of China-Africa Trade and Investment", "Research on Legal Risks of Investment Environment for Chinese Enterprises in Africa and the Countermeasures in the Context of the 'Belt and Road' Initiative", "History and Development of China-African Legal Cooperation", and "History of Legal Culture in Africa". The provincial and ministerial-level philosophy and social science planning projects mainly include "Research on the Legal System of African Human Rights Protection", "Research on African Investment Law", "African International Law: Achievements, Problems and Prospects", "Research on Environmental Law in South Africa", and "Research on African Regional Organization Law". The projects commissioned by national ministries and commissions mainly include "Research on Labor Disputes in China-Africa Production Capacity Cooperation", "Deficiencies of Existing China-Africa Bilateral Investment Treaties", and "African Countries' Jurisprudence and Socio-economic Development". The consultancy projects entrusted by enterprises mainly include "Guidelines for the Prevention of Legal Risks in Countries Along the 'Belt and Road' (South Africa)" and "Legal Consultation for Investment in South Africa".

II. Contact Information

Contact Person: Hong Yonghong; Tel: +86-731-58292281; Email: 3167381356@qq.com

Correspondence Address: Law School, Xiangtan University, Xuelin Road, Yuhu District, Xiangtan City, Hunan Province (411105), P. R. China.

Hunan African Cultural Research & Exchange Center, Changsha University of Science & Technology

I. Introduction

Hunan African Cultural Research & Exchange Center is a provincial-level think tank approved by the Foreign Affairs Office of the People's Government of Hunan Province in December 2013. It developed from the West African Culture Research Center at Changsha University of Science & Technology established in July 2012, and is affiliated to the School of Foreign Studies of the university. Professor Duan Shengfeng serves as the director.

The center is based on the Confucius Institute at the University of Liberia and committed to the studies of African culture as well as practice of cultural exchanges between China and Africa, with a view to providing auxiliary services for Hunan provincial government agencies in the activities of foreign affairs related to Africa, consultancy and translation services for various industries in Hunan in their exchanges with Africa, and consultancy and training services for local enterprises in their business development with Africa. Since its establishment, the center has kept pace with the times, forged ahead with determination, actively participated in the strategy of "Chinese Culture Going Global", and mainly conducted activities of theoretical research, practice and exchanges, and foreign affairs services.

The center has undertaken five projects of the National Social Science Fund of China, three projects of the Ministry of Education, and more than 10 projects of the Provincial Social Science Fund. It has published a total of 14 monographs, translations and compilations and more than 100 papers, over 30 of which were published on the journals of the Chinese Social Sciences Citation Index (CSSCI), and three of which were reproduced in the *Copy Edition of the Materials from Periodicals for Reference* of the Renmin University of China. After years of development, the center has formed stable research directions, covering the strategy of "Chinese Culture Going Global", education of African students in China, African literature (dramatic literature and oral literature), sustainable development of Confucius Institutes in Africa, and African English. *Into West Africa* published by the center was designated as the teaching material for the United Nations peacekeeping forces.

The center plays its role in serving the society mainly by supporting "Cultural

Ferrymen" volunteer service projects. Its volunteers are scattered all over the world, bringing Hunan influence everywhere. The volunteers can be seen at Confucius Institutes around the world, the China-Africa Economic and Trade Expo, the United Nations Center for Sustainable Agricultural Mechanization, the reception of foreign delegations to China, and other places. The "Cultural Ferryman" Volunteer Group for the International Promotion of Chinese Culture won the Gold Award in the third China Youth Volunteer Service Project Competition in 2016 (jointly hosted by the Central Committee of the Communist Youth League, the Central Spiritual Civilization Affairs Office, the Ministry of Civil Affairs, the Ministry of Water Resources, and other agencies), the eleventh China Young Volunteers "Outstanding Organization Award" and "Outstanding Project Award" (selected by the Central Committee of the Communist Youth League, the Ministry of Education, and other agencies) in 2016, and the first prize of outstanding achievements of the campus culture development in Hunan Province in 2017 (selected by Hunan Provincial Department of Education).

The center has successively undertaken two training programs for expatriates of China Energy Engineering Group Hunan Power Construction Co., Ltd., one training program for Portuguese-speaking talents of Guangxi Hydroelectric Construction Bureau, and one training program for local employees of China Road & Bridge Corporation Montenegro Branch, and held the "First Seminar on Translation and Teaching of Energy and Electricity as Well as Application of Information Technology". The center has selected 13 Chinese directors or instructors and 22 student volunteers to serve in Confucius Institutes or Confucius Classrooms in Liberia, Algeria, South Korea, Montenegro, Malaysia, Thailand and other countries. It has provided training for more than 30 language students of Liberia in China, and Samuel K Deyekeh has become the first native instructor of Chinese language in Liberia.

The center has established close ties with the Liberian educational community. It has received the educational delegation of the Foreign Service Institute of Liberia once, the educational delegation of the University of Liberia five times, the Liberian cultural delegation of the Confucius Institute summer camp six times, the US cultural delegation of the East Stroudsburg summer camp twice, and the cultural delegation of the Confucius Institute of Montenegro twice.

The center boasts a research team of strong research abilities, reasonable age structure, and high titles and degrees. There are three professors, five associate professors, and several lecturers in the team, and seven of them have gained doctoral degrees. The center has fixed offices and facilities, with one executive deputy director responsible for daily affairs. It also offers one or two positions for work-study students.

II. Contact Information

Contact Person: Liu Tanxiao; Tel: +86-731-85258545; Email: 32449147@qq.com

Correspondence Address: Room 613, Section A, Arts Building, School of Foreign Studies, Changsha University of Science & Technology, No. 960 Section Two of Wanjiali South Road, Tianxin District, Changsha City, Hunan Province, P. R. China.

Center of African Studies, Hunan Normal University

I. Introduction

The Center of African Studies at Hunan Normal University was established on the basis of the discipline of political science of the university, which could date back to the late 1930s. As one of the earliest universities in Hunan Province to carry out African studies, Hunan Normal University has conducted research on African politics, South Africa's constitution, culture of Francophone countries of Africa, and African tourism market. In 2007 and 2011, after the university's discipline of political science was approved as a post-doctoral research station and a first-level doctoral program in political science, African studies was listed as a specialized orientation of the major International Politics. In 2017, the Center of African Studies was officially established. In 2018, Changsha City of

Hunan Province was designated as the permanent host city of the "China-Africa Economic and Trade Expo" by the Ministry of Commerce. The center took the initiative to meet the actual needs of cooperation between Chinese and African provinces and cities, and actively built a think tank and exchange platform for African studies in central China. In the same year, the center held the "First Seminar on the 'Belt and Road' and the China-Africa Community with a Shared Future and the Unveiling Ceremony of the Center of African Studies of Hunan Normal University".

The Center of African Studies is a comprehensive teaching and research institution as well as a platform of academic exchanges and think tank for African studies and China-Africa cooperation in the central part of China. The center is committed to promoting cooperation between Hunan and Africa; conducting research mainly on the history of Africa and its individual countries, African law and humanities; and providing intellectual support and services for Hunan-Africa economic, trade and cultural cooperation.

Professor Chen Xiaohong serves as the director of the center. The research teams include the "Belt and Road" and China-Africa cooperation team, the China-Africa modern agriculture and animal husbandry cooperation team, the African legal and social research team, the China-Africa tourism and cultural and creative cooperation team, and the China-Africa people-to-people and cultural exchanges and language service team. There are 13 full-time and part-time researchers, including eight professors, one associate professor, and four young scholars under the age of 35. The center has also invited four famous researchers from home and abroad to join them as guest researchers.

In recent years, by taking the advantage of Hunan becoming the permanent host of the China-Africa Economic and Trade Expo, the center has held a series of academic conferences, lectures and exchanges with foreign countries; carried out a series of think tank research in collaboration with research experts in and out of Hunan on health, agricultural development, poverty alleviation, education and training, laws and regulations, pharmaceutical development, and other issues of China and Africa; and actively offered suggestions and proposals for government departments, enterprises and institutions, providing intellectual support and guarantee for China-Africa cooperation in trade, economy and exchanges.

With joint efforts of the team members, the center has participated in the research on the overall African history, including the multi-volume *Africa, Colonial History: African Volume*, and the multi-volume *African Economic History*; compiled and published a series of achievements on African country-specific studies: *Malawi, Swaziland,* and *Lesotho*; and published special research results such as *Research on the Innovation of China-Africa Bilateral Investment Treaties in the Context of the "Belt and One" Initiative*, *History of Legal Culture in Africa*, *Armed Groups' Motivation and Process of Norm Learning* and *Armed Conflicts and Resolutions in North Uganda.*

Relying on the university's first-level doctoral programs of political science and legal science, the center now offers specialized courses on the relationship between Africa and major countries as well as on overview of African studies. It also recruits master's and doctoral candidates of African studies in such programs as Theory of Political Science, International Politics, and International Law. Thus, the center has formed a relatively continuous talent fostering system and cultivated dozens of talents specializing in African studies and African affairs.

Next, the center will continue to take advantage of the mechanism of the China-Africa Economic and Trade Expo, fully utilize resources of Hunan, and devote itself to China-Africa cooperation. As a provincial university, it will give full play to the role of the think tank for China-Africa exchanges, conduct research on trade promotion, investment and publicity, agricultural technologies, energy and electric power, cooperative parks, infrastructure and financing cooperation between China and African countries, and carry out research on investment law, environmental law, trade law and labor law of African countries. Based on in-depth research on cultures of African countries, it will explore the feasibility of implementing Hunan-Africa cultural tourism projects, creating a Hunan-Africa media cooperation network, promoting the establishment of Hunan-Africa cultural centers in both regions, and make attempts to promote mutual visits of scholars.

II. Contact Information

Contact Person: Chen Xiaohong; Email: 306201502@qq.com

Correspondence Address: School of Public Administration, Hunan Normal University, No. 36 Lushan Road, Changsha City, Hunan Province, P. R. China.

China-Africa Economic and Trade Research Center, Hunan University

I. Introduction

As the first action of the first initiative among the "Eight Major Initiatives" of China-Africa cooperation proposed by President Xi Jinping, the "China-Africa Economic and Trade Expo" has been permanently settled in Changsha and will be held every two years. Taking this as an opportunity, Hunan University integrated the advantages of the national key discipline of international trade and Hunan Provincial Trade Research Base and established the China-Africa Economic and Trade Research Center in January 2019. The director of the center is Professor Xu Helian (director of the School of Economics & Trade of Hunan University, chief expert of the major project of the National Social Science Fund of China, and distinguished professor of Furong Scholar), and the deputy director is Professor Xiao Hao (deputy director of the School of Economics & Trade of Hunan University, member of the first batch of young top talents of think tanks of Hunan Province, member of the "Huxiang Talents" program). The members of the center include Professor Lai Mingyong (Chang Jiang Scholar of the Ministry of Education, and leader of a project sponsored by the "National Science Fund for Distinguished Young Scholars"), Professor Zhang Yabin (leading talent of philosophy and social sciences in the national Ten Thousand Talents Program, famed cultural master, and talent of the "Four-Batch" Talent Program), Zhu Shujin (chief expert of the major project of the National Social Science Fund of China), Professor Hou Junjun (chief expert of the major project of the National Social Science Fund of China), and Professor Luo Nengsheng (chief expert of the major project of the National Social Science Fund of China, and consultant of the

People's Government of Hunan Province).

The major goals of the center are to provide academic and intellectual support for the success of the China-Africa Economic and Trade Expo to serve the strategy of opening up and rising of Hunan Province, and explore the long-term economic and trade cooperation mechanism between China and Africa to serve the strategic vision of "co-building a China-Africa community with a shared future" proposed by General Secretary Xi Jinping. Meanwhile, the center aims to provide support for the formation of a national educational brand of "education and training for Africa" to inject new momentum into Hunan as a strong province in education.

In terms of its function, it aims to develop into a professional think tank of China-Africa economic and trade cooperation, remain committed to exploring, researching and refining long-term China-Africa economic and trade cooperation mechanisms, and promote the formation of a market-oriented innovation model of comprehensive cooperation between China and Africa in trade and economy. It also aims to develop into a professional comprehensive service platform for China-Africa trade and economy, setting up a platform of government-industry-university-research cooperation, and providing specialized services such as exhibition innovation, business consultancy, industrial cooperation, resident services, information services, and scientific and technological cooperation for government, market and enterprises. In addition, it aims to develop into a special talent training base for China-Africa trade and economic cooperation, innovate its talent fostering model, design high-quality courses on the theme of China-Africa trade and economy, create an all-round and whole-process theoretical and practical talent fostering system, and foster versatile and innovative talents in the fields of African trade and economy.

Now, the research center is being transformed by the People's Government of Hunan Province into a China-Africa Economic & Trade Cooperation Institute.

II. Contact Information

Website: http://cet.hnu.edu.cn/

WeChat Official Account: China-Africa-Yuelu

Contact Person: Xiao Hao; Email: xh_26@126.com

Correspondence Address: School of Economics & Trade, Campus of College of Finance and Economics, Hunan University, Xihu Street, Yuelu District, Changsha City, Hunan Province, P. R. China.

Center for China-Africa Cooperation and Development, Central South University

I. Introduction

The Center for China-Africa Cooperation and Development at the Central South University, established in May 2019, is affiliated to the College of Literature and Journalism of the university. Professor Bai Yin, dean of the college, serves as the director of the center. Guided by Xi Jinping Thought on Socialism with Chinese Characteristics for a New Era, and with the concept of building a community with a shared future for mankind, the center conducts research on China-Africa culture, economy, science and technology, education and other fields to serve the country's strategic needs of diplomacy and promote the building of the "Belt and Road". It also provides services such as resource development, economic and trade cooperation, transportation and medical cooperation with Africa, and forges a business card of "Chinese Culture Going Global" so as to build the connection of comprehensive cooperation and exchanges between China and Africa and provide intellectual and technological support for China-Africa exchanges and cooperation.

The development goal of the center is to strive to develop into a model key new-type think tank in Hunan Province, a national-level think tank, and an economic and trade cooperation booster. Since the establishment of the center, it has focused on the following aspects.

First, relying on the advantages of complete disciplines of Central South University, it integrates the faculty and related resources of multiple institutions in the fields of mining and metallurgical engineering, public health, transportation, cultural communication, language services, and studies of the Association of Southeast Asian Nations (ASEAN), coordinates experts from relevant departments of Hunan Province and other universities as well as well-known scholars from domestic universities and research institutions, and gradually attracts foreign experts to form a first-class expert and research team in China. Focusing on the research direction, researchers of the center conduct discussions on African studies, China-Africa exchanges and cooperation, and the spread of Chinese culture in Africa from the theoretical perspective, and explore practical ways to promote China-Africa resource development, transportation, economic and trade cooperation, education cooperation, health care, and cultural exchanges. Thus, the center has yielded relevant results including think tank reports, monographs and papers.

Second, taking the economic, trade and cultural exchanges between Hunan Province and African countries as the starting point, the center vigorously carries out economic and trade promotion activities and research. It has assisted the government to host the China-Africa Economic and Trade Expo. The center conducts research on the status and development trend of China-Africa economic and trade cooperation as well as hot-spot issues related to Africa and their international impacts, so as to provide not only a theoretical basis for the government's decision-making on Africa but also consultancy and cross-border investment training for related companies exploring the African market. Taking advantage of the university's disciplines, it carries out activities related to international capacity cooperation, mineral resource development and utilization, rail transit, civil engineering, road construction and others; coordinates and serves research cooperation projects by government departments and major enterprises including training programs to assist Africa; and organizes short-term technical training courses.

Third, taking the Confucius Institutes in Africa, Xiangya School of Medicine, and Hunan Children's Hospital as the mainstay, the center carries out activities of international education, medical cooperation and cultural exchanges. Through cultural training and research on health communication for corporate personnel going to Africa, it has improved their abilities of exchanges and negotiations, quality of cultural life, and awareness of safety and health. It has coordinated and assisted the training of African postgraduates studying in China, and established the cultural, economic and technological exchanges mechanism between Hunan and Africa, so as to promote the image of Hunan and boost the spread of Chinese culture overseas. The center has made policy suggestions to strengthen China-Africa exchanges and cooperation.

Fourth, the center has focused on China-Africa literature and cultural exchanges. In terms of language services, it continues to focus on training of personnel assisting foreign countries and China-Africa forums to provide language services and language support for economic and trade exchanges between Hunan and Africa, and promote cultural and literary exchanges between China and Africa.

The center currently has more than 10 researchers.

II. Contact Information

WeChat Official Account: jiankangfeizhou

Contact Person: Zhou Wenjuan; Email: wenddi.zhou@csu.edu.cn

Correspondence Address: College of Literature and Journalism, Central South University, Lushan South Road, Changsha City, Hunan Province (410012), P. R. China.

China-Africa Economic and Trade Promotion Council

I. Introduction

In June 2019, the first China-Africa Economic and Trade Expo was held in Changsha, and it is supposed to become a regular event in Hunan. In September 2020, the China (Hunan) Free Trade Pilot Zone was approved. It will take economic and trade cooperation with Africa as one of the three key tasks and vigorously promote the building of a China-Africa In-depth Economic and Trade

Cooperation Pilot Zone. Under this context, the China-Africa Economic and Trade Promotion Council was established in Hunan Province. The council is a non-profit social organization voluntarily joined by enterprises, institutions and social organizations engaged in China-Africa economic and trade cooperation as well as experts and scholars who have gained some influence in the field of China-Africa economic and trade cooperation.

The council aims to build a "four-in-one bank" of ideas, talents, projects and practice cases, and establish a platform promoting the transformation of research results, economic and trade exchanges and cooperation, project development and matchmaking, and cultivation of market-oriented operations for in-depth economic and trade cooperation between China and Africa. Its core tasks include (1) serving the China-Africa Economic and Trade Expo in the aspects of preparation and follow-up project implementation, (2) providing support for the China-Africa In-depth Economic and Trade Cooperation Pilot Zone in terms of business promotion and professional service, and (3) exploring innovative models for local economic and trade cooperation with Africa.

The council hires three academicians, namely Yuan Longping, Chen Xiaohong and Liu Zhonghua, as well as two well-known scholars, namely He Maochun and Wang Tong, as chief experts, and sets up a research think tank composed of 35 experts from all fields. Both China Development Research Institute and the Foreign Affairs Research Center of Tsinghua University designate the council as their China-Africa economic and trade research base to carry out in-depth think tank research on economic and trade cooperation with Africa, provide economic and trade advisories for the government and enterprises, explore new approaches and new models for local economic and trade cooperation with Africa, establish demonstration projects and practice plans, and provide reliable decision-making foundations and feasible operational solutions for the establishment of a new platform for local cooperation with Africa and the promotion of high-quality development of China-Africa cooperation. The council will successively initiate "ten key projects" under the program of the China-Africa In-depth Economic and

Trade Cooperation Pilot Zone and the program of foreign economic and trade cooperation, solve significant theoretical and practical problems confronted during the building of the China (Hunan) Free Trade Pilot Zone, especially in the building of the China-Africa In-depth Economic and Trade Cooperation Pilot Zone, and explore to establish "more convenient" mechanism and policy framework for China-Africa economic and trade cooperation under WTO rules.

The council will, in accordance with the principle of "government guidance and market operation", and relying on the two state-level platforms of the China-Africa Economic and Trade Expo and the China-Africa In-depth Economic and Trade Cooperation Pilot Zone, build a leading comprehensive service institution in China for the promotion of China-Africa economic cooperation, which is centered in Hunan, leading the surrounding area influencing the whole country and benefiting the whole world. The council intends to build seven service systems, including a digital system of the whole industry, a full-chain financial support system, a three-dimensional logistics system, an overall market-oriented service system, a precise policy support system, a smooth trade and investment system, and a government-research-commerce integrated promotion system; establish 10 service centers including an advisory center, a resident center, a legal center, a foreign trade center, a language center, an exhibition center, and a fostering center for Chinese and African overseas students; provide "comprehensive and overall" one-stop service for enterprises engaged in economic and trade cooperation with Africa; promote the integration-oriented innovation of the service model in the China-Africa Economic and Trade Cooperation Promotion Innovation Demonstration Park, and gradually build a provincial, national or even international China-Africa economic and trade integrated service platform.

The main functions of the council are: (1) to strengthen project research and provide economic and trade advisories; (2) to set up a research platform and play a role in integration; (3) to organize various activities including seminars; (4) to collect market information and provide professional services; (5) to organize mutual visits and conduct mutual exchanges; (6) to carry out specialized training and foster economic and trade talents; and (7) to expand membership coverage and promote publicity.

The highest authority of the council is its General Assembly. The Board and the Standing Committee elected by the Board are the executive bodies of the General Assembly. Under the Board and its Standing Committee are a Secretariat consisting of project matchmaking posts, exhibition service posts, member service posts, a financial office and a general office. A number of professional committees and the ten service centers are responsible for the business of the council.

II. Contact Information

Contact Person: Liu Wen; Tel: +86-731-85986178; Fax: +86-731-85986178

Email: info@caetp.net.cn; Website: http://www.caetp.net.cn

WeChat Official Account: gh_0b8ed3da2ec5

Correspondence Address: Level 6, China-Africa Economic and Trade Cooperation Promotion Innovation Demonstration Park, Yuhua District, Changsha City, Hunan Province (410016), P. R. China.

China-Africa Agricultural Development and Cooperation Base, Hunan Agricultural University

I. Introduction

The China-Africa Agricultural Development and Cooperation Base is based on the School of Economics of Hunan Agricultural University (HUNAU) and is subordinate to the China-Africa Economic & Trade Research Institute. The base aims at cutting-edge theory and technology research, focuses on agricultural science and technology, integrates domestic and foreign agricultural technology and expert resources, and meets major strategic needs of the country. It is a platform for research on real-life issues of transnational cooperation in "soft power" between China and Africa, such as agricultural production technology, agricultural management system, agricultural standards. The base focuses its efforts on solving the problems of information, capital and service faced by agricultural technology, agricultural talents, agriculture-related industries, enterprises and products going abroad. It provides intellectual support and decision-making reference for building a new model of China-Africa agricultural economic and trade cooperation, promoting the high-quality development of China-Africa agricultural economic and trade cooperation, the "Belt and Road Initiative", and accelerating the building of a closer community with a shared future for China and Africa. The base consists of three centers: China-Africa Agricultural Technology Development and Cooperation Research Center, China-Africa Agricultural Cooperation Information and Data Center, and China-Africa Agricultural Talent fostering and Technology Innovation Center.

With the implementation of the "Eight Major Initiatives" in collaboration with African countries and the "Belt and Road Initiative", China-Africa economic and trade cooperation has entered a new stage. The First China-Africa Economic and Trade Expo was successfully held in Changsha, Hunan Province in June 2019 and the expo site has been permanently settled in Changsha. The holding of the expo and the approval of China (Hunan) Pilot Free Trade Zone have brought unprecedented opportunities for the agricultural development and cooperation between Hunan and Africa. Approved by the Department of Commerce of Hunan Province, China-Africa Economic & Trade Research Institute was finally established by Hunan University, with Mr. He Baoxiang, Vice Governor of Hunan Province, as the dean, and chairmen of the University Affairs Committees from Hunan University, Xiangtan University, HUNAU, and Central South University as the vice deans. "China-Africa Economic and Trade Research Base", "Xiangtan University Base for China-Africa Law and Humanities", "China-Africa Agricultural Development and Cooperation Base", and "China-Africa Mining Cooperation Research Base" were established at the four universities respectively. On the morning of August 23, 2020, the China-Africa Agricultural Development and Cooperation Base was officially unveiled at HUNAU. The base has the following characteristics.

The expert committee of the base, led by the academicians of HUNAU, with academician Liu Zhonghua as the director of the expert advisory committee, and Yuan Longping, Guan Chunyun, Yin Yilong, Liu Zhonghua, Liu Shaojun, Yuan Yanwen, XuXiangping, Bo Lianyang, Wang Kling, Lv Zheng, Guo Kesha, Jiang Heping, Lu Fucai, Li Zuojun, Rui Mingjie, Liu Youjin, Yang Jinqiang and Lu Lei as the members of the advisory committee, strives to build a platform of top experts and provide intellectual support for China-Africa agricultural development and cooperation.

The three centers established in the base, namely China-Africa Agricultural Cooperation Information and Data Center, China-Africa Agricultural Technology Development and Cooperation Research Center, and China-Africa Agricultural Talent Cultivation and Technology Innovation Center, form a core platform for academic research and industry exchanges on agricultural development and cooperation between China and Africa.

The development objectives of the base are: (1) to build a high-end think tank of theoretical and technical support for China-Africa agricultural cooperation. In correspondence with the strategic needs of the "Belt and Road Initiative", the cooperation with African countries and the demand of Hunan's opening up and rising, the base aims to build a high-end think tank of cutting-edge agricultural theory and technology support for China-Africa agricultural cooperation. It digs deep into the advantageous resources of agricultural science of HUNAU and carries out research on science and technology around the frontier basic theory and key engineering technology in China-Africa agricultural cooperation. The base strives to make a number of major and original theoretical achievements and provide strong theoretical and technical support for the promotion of China-Africa agricultural cooperation and the "Belt and Road" construction. (2) to build a resource integration and exchange center for China-Africa agricultural cooperation. Taking advantage of the new research base and the two platforms of China-Africa Economic and Trade Expo and China (Hunan) Pilot Free Trade Zone, the base deepens the synergy and cooperation with top research institutions at home and abroad, expands cooperation with the International Commission of

Agricultural Engineering, the Consultative Group on International Agricultural Research, the International Fund for Agricultural Development, the Food and Agriculture Organization, and the World Bank, and integrates international academic resources, so as to build a platform for exchanges and cooperation in the field of agriculture between China and Africa, and seize the opportunities of international agricultural technology innovation. (3) to build a center of agricultural talent fostering and technology innovation for China and Africa. In line with the international governance model and operational mechanism, the base explores the establishment of a world-class training model to cultivate and reserve a group of young leading talents in the field of agricultural technology to provide talent support for China-Africa agricultural cooperation. At the same time, it carries out high-end agricultural technology training programs and foster the mainstay of African agricultural technology, so as to turn the China-Africa Agricultural Development and Cooperation Base into an incubation base for international agricultural technology talents and a center for fostering high-end agricultural talents and technological innovation.

II. Contact Information

Contact Person: Wen Chunhui; Tel: +86-731-84618197; Email: Wchui0207@163.com

Correspondence Address: School of Economics, Hunan Agricultural University, No. 1 Nongda Road, Furong District, Changsha City, Hunan Province (410128), P. R. China.

Center of African Studies, Nanjing University

I. Introduction

The Center of African Studies at Nanjing University is the first specialized institution in China to systematically study the economic development of Africa from the perspective of geography. Its predecessor was the “Research Institute of African Economic Geography of Nanjing University” approved by the

Ministry of Higher Education in 1964. In 1993, it was renamed the Center of African Studies under the approval of the Ministry of Education. In 2013, the Center of African Studies (Research Center) of Nanjing University was included in the base development of international research centers at universities in Jiangsu Province.

After more than fifty years, the center has shaped its tradition and distinctive advantage: based on academic research, focusing on the fostering of talents, and actively serving the development of national and local cooperation with Africa. Its aims to develop into an African research base with international influence and domestic characteristics as well as a training base for high-level talents of African studies in China.

In the 21st century, with the strengthening of China-Africa cooperation, the Center of African Studies has continuously strengthened academic research and served national strategies, and has formed the development philosophy of focusing on the fostering of talents and actively serving national strategies on the basis of academic research. Nanjing University has gathered together its strengths to form a research team of African studies with a combination of full-time and part-time researchers. At present, the center is headed by Professor Zhang Zhenke, with Associate Professor Liu Litao as its deputy director. The main researchers, with their research fields, include Professor Liu Chengfu (French literature, Francophone countries of Africa, and China-French-African cooperation), Professor Zhen Feng (African urbanization), Professor Huang Xianjin (African land resources), Professor Zhang Jinhe (tourism geography), Professor Huang Fanhua (international trade, globalization, and industrial chains), Associate Professor Zhao Shuhe (African arid agriculture and remote sensing), and Associate Professor Zhang Xingqi (African water resources). With strong support of Nanjing University, the center has also hired Ambassador Zhong Jianhua and Ambassador Sun Shuzhong, who had worked in the front line of Africa, as part-time/guest professors to direct and participate in the research. Relevant entrepreneurs involved in investment and trade in Africa are also hired as part-time researchers of the center. From 2018 to 2019, the center introduced two full-time researchers and established a post-doctoral research station, continuously strengthening its team of African studies.

The Center of African Studies boasts profound and unique characteristics, upholds the tradition of "Sincerity with Aspiration, Perseverance with Integrity", and has achieved fruitful academic results. It has won a number of awards of second-prize or above in philosophy, humanities and social sciences from the Ministry of Education and Jiangsu Province. From 1964 to 1965, the internal journal *African Economic Geographical Reference Materials* was published. In 1973, it was renamed *African Geographical Materials*, with the volume number continued. As of 1984, a total of 27 issues had been published, covering geostrategy, steel industry, petroleum geography, agricultural geography and other issues of almost all countries in Africa. In the mid-1980s, Nanjing University had nearly 20 full-time researchers and assistants in African economic geography, with outstanding achievements in African research. The *Atlas of African Geography,* known as China's "Encyclopedia of African Studies", was published in 1985, which contains maps, thematic maps and text explanations of more than 600,000 words. From the 1980s to the early 1990s, Nanjing University published *General Introduction to World Agricultural Geography*, *African Petroleum Geography*, *African Physical Geography*, *African Agricultural Geography*, and other books as well as serial internal materials *Special Report of African Geography*. The book *African Economic and Social Development Strategy Research* edited by Professor Zhang Tongzhu of Nanjing University in the 1990s embodies the consensus of multiple scholars and is a classic work of China's African research. The book won the second prize of the first Outstanding Achievements in Humanities and Social Sciences of the Ministry of Education. In 2019, the center published the *Collection of African Economic Geography and Regional Development Research Materials* (Volume I-VI), which is a collection of internal research results of African geography of Nanjing University from 1964 to 1985. The series contains valuable historical materials on China's African studies and is conducive to

African studies from unique perspectives. Since 2012, it has published numerous research results including *African Agriculture Pictorials*, *African Land Resources and Food Security*, *African Human Geography*, *African Port Economy and Urban Development*, *African Fishery Resources and Development Strategy Research*, *African Agriculture and Rural Development*, *Research on China-Africa Cooperation and Energy Security Strategy*, *Africa Overview and China-Africa Cooperation*, and *The Golden Rhinoceros: Histories of the Africa Middle Ages*. Related research results have won the second prize of the Philosophy and Social Sciences Outstanding Achievement Award of the Ministry of Education and Jiangsu Province. The Center of African Studies also actively serves the society, providing relevant consultancy services for national and local departments and enterprises.

The center attaches great importance to specialized training of African research talents. In terms of training master's and doctoral candidates, the relevant majors include Geography, Foreign Languages and Literature, Marine Science, International Relations, International Politics, International Economics and Trade, and others.

In recent years, the center has attached great importance to academic exchanges and cooperation with Africa. It has maintained close contact and cooperation with experts and scholars from Emory University (the United States), the University of Tübingen (Germany), Cairo University (Egypt), Kenyatta University (Kenya), the Development Research Institute at Sokoine University of Agriculture (Tanzania), the Institute of Marine Sciences at the University of Dar es Salaam (Tanzania), the Research Center for Applied Economics for Development (Algeria), the University of Cape Town (South Africa), the Center of Africa and Asia Studies (Morocco), Mohammed V University (Morocco), Hawassa University (Ethiopia), Addis Ababa University (Ethiopia), and the Institute for Euro-African Studies of Hanyang University (South Korea). Since 2005, Nanjing University has hosted "Going to Africa, Seeking Development" Forum four times and multiple international conferences related to the development of Africa. In recent years, the center has initiated the program of "Partnership of African Development Studies" and has participated in the hosting of two consecutive "African Development and Asian-African Cooperation International Symposiums" (in Morocco and South Korea respectively). In 2019, the center co-organized the "Second Jiangsu-SADC High Level Forum for Investment and Development", and more than 300 guests from home and abroad attended the conference.

II. Contact Information

Website: http://iasnju.nju.edu.cn/

WeChat Official Account: casnju

Contact Person: Zhang Zhenke; Tel: +86-25-89686604

Correspondence Address: Center of African Studies, Nanjing University, No. 163 Kunshan Building, Xianlin Road, Nanjing City, Jiangsu Province (210023), P. R. China.

Institute of Asian and African Studies, Jiangsu Normal University

I. Introduction

The Institute of Asian and African Studies at Jiangsu Normal University was established in 1993, and its predecessor was the Office of Asian and African Studies established in 1987. Taking the comprehensive regional research in the Asian-African region as the target, the institute mainly conducts research on the current situation of economy, politics and international relations of the Asian and African regions and countries, as well as the academic fields of history, society, culture, ethnicity and religion. Since the beginning of the 21st century, with the continuous expansion and deepening of reform and opening up, the institute's development has been highly valued by the university, and its research abilities have been continuously strengthened. It has made great progress and in 2006 it was upgraded to a university-level research institute.

The institute currently has 12 full-time and part-time teachers and researchers, including eight professors, three associate professors, and one lecturer. Among them, seven have docotral degrees, two are doctoral advisors, and five are master's advisors. Most of the researchers of the institute have had training experiences at home and abroad. The insitute is committed to conducting academic exchanges with famous universities including Peking University and Nanjing University, and has established ties with several world-renowned universities. It plays an active role in participating in relevant activities organized by the Chinese Society of African Historical Studies and the Chinese Society of Asian and African Studies.

Relying on the master's programs of World History and Specialized History offered by the School of History, Culture and Tourism at Jiangsu Normal University, the institute has conducted activities such as holding academic lectures and hosting or participating in academic conferences, producing wide and positive influences among students and academia. For example, the annual meeting of the Chinese Society of African Historical Studies was held at Jiangsu Normal University three times, among which the eighth annual meeting and China-Africa Relations Seminar was the first annual meeting after the FOCAC Beijing Summit, with unprecedented success. Participants of the annual meeting included academic colleagues from universities and research institutions, government officials responsible for China-Africa exchange affairs from the Development Research Center of the State Council, the Ministry of Foreign Affairs, and the Ministry of Education, as well as senior executives from enterprises and institutions such as the China Africa Investment Network and Shanghai World Expo Coordination Bureau. The meeting was fully covered by mainstream media such as *People's Daily* and major websites, and exerted considerable influence overseas.

In recent years, the institute has led and finished a number of projects of the National Social Science Fund of China, the Planning Projects of the Ministry of Education and Jiangsu Provincial Government, the Major Projects of Philosophy and Social Sciences of Universities in Jiangsu Province, and university-level research projects. A considerable number of academic achievements were published every year. The main research results involving African studies include the National Social Science Fund Later-Period Sponsoring Project "Land Issues and South Africa's Economy and Politics" and the general project of the National Social Science Fund of China "Research on Racial Reconciliation in South Africa", both led by Professor Sun Hongqi, director of the institute. Professor Sun Hongqi published the *Monograph on Colonialism and Africa,* which won the third prize of the 11th Jiangsu Provincial Government's Outstanding Achievements in Philosophy and Social Sciences, and *Land Issues and South Africa's Politics and Economy,* which won the second prize of the 12th Jiangsu Provincial Government's Outstanding Achievements in Philosophy and Social Sciences. In addition, Professor Sun Hongqi also participated in the research work *History of Colonialism (African Volume)* of the National Philosophy and Social Science Planning Project led by Peking University and the key project of the Social Science Research Fund of the Ministry of Education, and the translation of the *General History of Africa*, a project sponsored by the United Nations Educational, Scientific and Cultural Organization (UNESCO). Currently, Professor Sun Hongqi is the vice president of the Chinese Society of African Historical Studies and a council member of the Chinese Society of Asian and African Studies. In addition to fundamental research, Professor Sun Hongqi and his colleagues also pay attention to the application of research results to serve the country's high-end strategies and local economic and social development goals. Their research results on China-Africa cooperation and other related issues under the "Belt and Road" Initiative have been adopted and approved by the Chinese People's Political Consultative Conference (CPPCC) and state leaders.

II. Contact Information

Contact Person: Sun Hongqi; Tel: +86-516-83403258; Email: hongqisun@126.com

Correspondence Address: No. 101 Shanghai Road, Tongshan New District, Xuzhou City, Jiangsu Province (221116), P. R. China.

Center for African Agriculture Studies, Nanjing Agricultural University

I. Introduction

Nanjing Agricultural University (NAU)boasts a long history of cooperation with Africa and has achieved remarkable results. In 1995, it signed a university-level cooperation agreement with Egerton University of Kenya. From 1995 to 2002, NAU and Egerton University implemented three phases of the China-Kenya Agreement for Cooperation in Higher Education, and the China-Kenya Horticulture Technical Cooperation Center was established in Kenya. In 1998, President Daniel Arap Moi of Kenya paid an inspection to the China-Kenya Horticulture Technical Cooperation Center. In 2004, NAU undertook its first program of Chinese aid to Africa in training of agricultural technology sponsored by the Ministry of Education. In 2006, it undertook its first program of Chinese aid to Africa in training of agricultural technology sponsored by the Ministry of Commerce. In the same year, the Center for African Agriculture Studies was established, and in 2008, the center was approved by the Ministry of Education as one of the first batch of Bases of Educational Aid to Foreign Countries. Also in 2008, the first overseas agricultural technology training class was opened in Kenya. In 2010, NAU and Egerton University joined the "China-Africa Universities 20+20 Cooperation Plan" of the Ministry of Education. In 2012, NAU awarded an honorary doctorate to Vice President Kalonzo Musyoka of Kenya,and in cooperation with Egerton University, built a Confucius Institute featuring agricultural studies. In 2014, the construction of the "China-Kenya Agricultural Demonstration Park" was started. In 2016, with the approval and sponsoring of the Ministry of Science and Technology, the Kenya-China Joint Laboratory for Crop Molecular Biology was established. In 2019, the laboratory was upgraded and listed in the first "Belt and Road"Joint Laboratories of the country. In 2017, the Agricultural Technology Training Alliance for Confucius Institutes in Africa was set up under the initiative of NAU.

The center implements the "Belt and Road" Initiative of the country and carries out scientific research, talent fostering and technology promotion through integration of full-time and part-time personnel, interdisciplinary cooperation between natural sciences and social sciences, and combination of domestic research with overseas research(field studies in Africa). It focuses its research on major theoretical and practical issues in Africa's agricultural reform and development, and provides scientific analysis, advisory and services for the government's formulation of policies and plans on China-Africa agricultural cooperation and the "going global" of China's agriculture. By exploring major theoretical and practical issues in the agricultural reform and development of African countries, the center forster high-end talents for agricultural production and development of African countries; disseminates advanced and applicable Chinese agricultural technology to African countries; and promotes the implementation of the "Belt and Road" Initiative, the building of a community of a shared future for China and Africa, and the "going global" of China's agriculture.

The center has undertaken more than 10 international cooperation projects of South-South Cooperation and "948" Program of the Ministry of Agriculture; conducting research on food security and poverty reduction, utilization of agricultural resources, agricultural investment, and development of agricultural science and technology in African countries, rendering technological and administrative support for agricultural modernization of African countries, and providing advisory for the Chinese government and enterprises on cooperation with Africa. In 2018, two special programs, namely Special Program on China-Africa Cooperation and Exchange and Special Program on Country-Specific Studies of African Countries, were set up under the university-level International Cooperation Capacity Enhancement Program. Eight projects including "Studies of China-East Africa Transfer Path of Rice Cultivation Technology" and "Highly Effective Utilization of Crude Feed Resources for Ruminants in China and Africa" have been approved and funded. In 2008, 2010 and 2012, the center held three consecutive sessions of the "Exploring Africa and Seeking Development" Forum in cooperation with the Center of African Studies at Nanjing University and other institutions, edited and published three *Essay Compilations of the Exploring Africa and Seeking Development Forum*. The forum has become a key platform for experts from domestic universities and research institutions to conduct research and exchanges on African issues, particularly on agricultural issues. The center has planned abook series of*Agricultural Development and Practical Technology in Africa*,among which *Farming in Nigeria* and *Farming in Kenya* have been officially published, and *Farming in Ethiopia*,*Farming in Tanzania*, *Farming in Sudan*, and *Farming in Rwanda* are in the process of compilation.

The center brings its disciplinary advantages into play and forsters innovative talents. Taking Kenya as an example, between 2003 and 2019, a total of 98 Kenyan students, including those seeking college degrees and those for long-term training, were enrolled, among which 52 were doctoral candidates and 35 were master's candidates, covering more than 30 majors includingagronomy, biology, environmental science and engineering, and agricultural economics and management. In 2017, the center gained the approval of a Center of Excellence for Sustainable Agriculture and Agricultural Business Management by the World Bank, and plans to jointly forster 90 modern agricultural science and technology talents at the doctoral and master's levels. The project has also received the attention of the International Livestock Research Institute, and the three sides will combine their advantages in resources to jointly conduct talent forstering and scientific research and provide intellectual support for the promotion of African development. NAUhas also sent agricultural experts to Kenya to carry out technical training and demonstration. From 2012 to 2019, 28 training classes were heldoverscas on greenhouse technology, semi-arid agricultural production technology, and agricultural product quality and safety,benefiting more than 1,000 trainees.

II. Contact Information

Contact Person: Yao Hong; Tel: +86-25-84396489; Email: hyao@njau.edu.cn

Correspondence Address: Room D417, North Wing, Administration Building,

College of International Education, Nanjing Agricultural University,No. 6Tongwei Road, Xuanwu District, Nanjing City, Jiangsu Province (210095), P. R. China.

Center for Sudanese Studies, Yangzhou University

I. Introduction

In the 1970s, Yangzhou University began to provide educational and scientific research assistance to Africa. In 2008, Yangzhou University held the first "China-Arab (10+1) Higher Education Cooperation Seminar" of the Ministry of Education, and set the goal of focusing on educational and research assistance to Africa and carrying out African regional and country-specific studies. In 2009, representatives of Yangzhou University attended the "Seminar on China-Arab Higher Education and Scientific Research Cooperation" held in Khartoum, Sudan. They proposed for the first time to conduct educational and research cooperation as well as country-specific studies with Sudan as the key target country. In 2010, Yangzhou University and Khartoum University joined the "China-Africa Universities 20+20 Cooperation Plan" of the Ministry of Education in pairs, formally specifying Sudan as the target country to carry out educational and research cooperation as well as regional and country-specific studies. In 2012, the Center for African Studies (Center for Sudanese Studies) of Yangzhou University and the China-Sudan Joint Research and Exchange Center of Modern Agriculture Technology of Yangzhou University were formally founded. In 2017, the Center for Sudanese Studies was approved as a Regional and Country-Specific Studies Center Registered with the Ministry of Education, and held the 2017 General Meeting of the Chinese Society of African Historical Studies and the Academic Conference of "the 'Belt and Road' Initiative and African Development". In 2018, the center introduced full-time researchers and hosted the first "High-Level Forum on China-Sudan Relations and Academic Seminar on Sudan Issues". In 2019, it participated in the International Symposium of "History, Current Status and Outlook of China-Sudan Relations" and the Seminar of "China-Sudan Relations and Sudan's Political, Diplomatic and Economic Policies" in Khartoum. It also co-hosted the "China-Sudan Forum on Development of Higher Education Cooperation" with the College for Overseas Education. On November 25, 2019, the Center for South Sudanese Studies of Yangzhou University was founded.

Focusing on the "Belt and Road" Initiative and the strategic needs of building a China-Africa community with a shared future, the center conducts a full range of fundamental and practical research on Sudan, with "Sudan's national conditions" and "China-Sudan cooperation" as two major academic research areas. It also carries out regional studies on the neighboring countries of Sudan, North Africa and the Horn of Africa.

Professor Yu Hongliang, vice president of Yangzhou University, serves as the director of the center. Professor Wang Jinquan, dean of the College of International Studies, serves as the executive director. Dr. Jiang Hengkun, an expert on Sudanese issues, is a distinguished academic consultant and researcher at the center. In 2018, the center introduced four full-time researchers and formed a core research team with researchers from the departments of Arabic, French, English, and others. At present, the center has 17 full-time researchers, including two researchers from Sudan.

Since 2014, the center has been granted 20 projects of different levels and types, including four provincial and ministerial projects. On September 10, 2018, its WeChat official account "Center for Sudanese Studies at Yangzhou University" was opened to the public, and 97 articles have been published by the end of 2019. In 2019, the center submitted 31 research results, completed 10 research projects and one manual on Sudanese education, and published nine research papers. Meanwhie, the center conducted a number of investigations, invited experts to give lectures, and published opinions on the development of Sudan through multiple channels.

Based on the undergraduate major of Arabic, the center recruits graduate students of "regional and country-specific studies" in the majors of Arabic Language and Literature, French Language and Literature, and Foreign

Linguistics and Applied Linguistics. With "China-Sudan Joint Research and Exchange Center of Modern Agriculture Technology at Yangzhou University" as the base, it conducts agricultural exchanges and cooperation with Sudan and cultivates master's and doctoral students. It offers specialized training under the framework of the "China-Africa Universities 20+20 Cooperation Plan" of the Ministry of Education. By 2019, nearly 800 Sudanese students had participated in the training programs in China. It has also established joint training programs with Khartoum University and other cooperative institutions in Sudan, forming a relatively systematic talent fostering system.

The center adopts a development strategy of combinging "going out" with "bringing in", attaches great importance to field research in Sudan and the utilization of foreign research achievements, and establishes close cooperative relations with major foreign institutes of Sudanese studies. It has established contact with two major international academic institutions of Sudanese studies, namely, the Sudan Studies Society of the UK (SSSUK) and the Sudan Studies Association of North America (SSA); reached consensus and signed cooperation agreements with 11 universities in Sudan (and South Sudan); set up close cooperative relations with the Ministry of Higher Education and Scientific Research of Sudan, the Ministry of Water Resources and Irrigation of Egypt, and the National Research Center of Egypt; and maintained close ties with world renowned pollsters Gallop, Inc. and Pew Research Center as well as leading Sudanese think tanks (African Center for International Studies, Arrakaiz International Training Center, and the Ebony Center for Strategic Studies), conducting regular exchanges and discussions with them on regional relations, situations in Northeast Africa, higher education, agricultural cooperation and others.

With academic research as the core and disciplinary construction and personnel training as the foundation, the center aims to develop into a well-known regional and country-specific studies center integrating academic research, talent cultivation, social services and international exchanges, so as to serve the needs of the country and society. Its core pursuits are to promote mutual understanding between the Chinese and Sudanese peoples, foster talents with knowledge about specific countries, regions and fields, and provide intellectual support for the development of China-Sudan, China-Africa, China-Arab relations as well as the construction of the "Belt and Road".

II. Contact Information

Website: http://sdyjzx.yzu.edu.cn/

WeChat Official Account: SudaneseStudies

Contact Person: Wang Jinquan; Tel: +86-514-87971608; Email: bfsuwjq@163.com

Correspondence Address: Duxing Building, Yangzijin Campus, Yangzhou University, No. 196 Huayang West Road, Yangzhou City, Jiangsu Province, P. R. China.

Center of Africa Studies with the Belt and Road, Changzhou Academy of Social Sciences

I. Introduction

The Center of Africa Studies with the Belt and Road was co-founded by Changzhou Academy of Social Sciences, Changzhou Bureau of Commerce, Changzhou Economic and Information Commission and Hohai University on March 8, 2017. It aims to further enhance the advantage of new think tank building, strengthen the collaborative innovation of government-industry-university-research cooperation, better serve China-Africa capacity cooperation under the "Belt and Road" Initiative and the construction of the "Belt and Road" intersection in Jiangsu Province, and foster the advantage of Changzhou's opening up.The center gives full play to the discipline advantages of Hohai University; consolidates the research strength in the fields of water resources, water conservancy and hydropower, environmental engineering, transportation, energy, logistics network engineering, management science and business administration; and by pooling the wisdom of all parties,works to build a first-class strategic think tank of African studies in China on the basis of existing social science think tanks, so as to provide intellectual support for Jiangsu Province and Changzhou City to integrate into the building of the "Belt and Road" Initiative and enhance the internationalization level of enterprises.

By integrating all resources of the society, the center undertakes special projects of Changzhou Academy of Social Sciences, Changzhou Bureau of Commerce and Changzhou Economic and Information Commission every year. Meanwhile, it conducts research on African economy, culture, environment, and society, and strives to produce high-quality research results to provide theoretical guidance for the construction of the "Belt and Road" and international capacity cooperation in Changzhou. It strives to build a practical, innovative and responsible center with the vision of satisfying the needs of the country, serving the opening up and development, and enhancing China-Africa friendship. With the goal of serving the Changzhou government, enterprises and institutions and the "first-class discipline" construction of Hohai University, it provides theoretical guidance and technical support for Changzhou to promote the construction of the "Belt and Road" and international capacity cooperation, and offers Jiangsu (Changzhou) enterprises intellectual support and consultancy services in talent cultivation, international exchanges, foreign-related laws, and policy consultancy regarding investment and capacity cooperation with Africa, making contributions to China's "going global" strategy and direct investment to foreign countries.

The center conducts prospective and strategic studies on China's opening up policy and the construction of the "Belt and Road" Initiative. It undertakes major projects of the National Social Science Fund of China, projects of the National Natural Science Foundation of China, projects of Social Science Foundation of Jiangsu Province, projects of the Social Science Fund of the Ministry of Education, and science and technology supporting projects of Changzhou City. Focusing on China-Africa trade and investment, opening up and the "going global" strategy, the center summarizes and spreads the achievements and experience of China (Jiangsu Province) in opening up and international cooperation. Centering around facilitating the construction of the "Belt and Road" intersection, it studies the direction and focus of industrial transfer and international capacity cooperation in Jiangsu Province (Changzhou City); explores cooperation of international capacity between China and Africa, the construction of overseas production and innovation parks, and the pilot construction of global industrial science and technology innovation centers; undertakes major research projects and science and technology supporting projects; and provides theoretical support and decision-making consultancy services. The center is committed to the following fields of studies: (1) China-Africa trade and investment, including research on African trade and investment as well as research and consultancy on African trade and investment policies; (2) water resources in Africa, including research on water resources in Africa as well as research and consultancy on policies for the development and utilization of water resources in Africa; (3) infrastructure connectivity construction in Africa, including research on infrastructure connectivity construction as well as research on policies for Chinese enterprises to participate in infrastructure construction in Africa; and (4) China (Changzhou)-Africa people-to-people and educational exchanges, including research on educational and people-to-people exchanges between Chinese and African universities as well as research and consultancy on China (Changzhou)-Africa people-to-people and educational exchange policies.

Since its establishment, the center has actively conducted academic exchanges and research projects, undertaken research projects of the National Social Science Fund of China such as "Research on Strategic Adjustment, Aggregation and Governance of Chinese Enterprises' Overseas Investment in Africa from the Perspective of Spatial Economics" and "Research on Knowledge Transfer Mechanism, Path and Countermeasures of 'Going Global' of China's High-Speed Railway Standards from the Perspective of Global Value Chain", and sent researchers to visit South Africa, Sudan and Ethiopia. It has conducted key research projects commissioned by Changzhou Academy of Social Sciences including "Research on Changzhou's Docking International Capacity Transfer and African Cooperation" and "Research on the Belt and Road Initiative and Changzhou's Opening-up Development". It has complied multiple important research reports and proposals and published a series of academic papers in core journals such as *Jiangsu Social Sciences*, *Economic Review Journal*, and *Modern Economic Research*. It has invited multiple well-known domestic experts on African studies to give guidance and academic lectures. Meanwhile, some of its experts and scholars have actively participated in important domestic academic conferences to carry out academic exchanges and achievement sharing.

II. Contact Information

Website: http://bs.hhuc.edu.cn/

Contact Person: Tian Ze; Email: tianze21@126.com

Correspondence Address: No. 200 Jinling North Road, Changzhou City, Jiangsu Province (213022), P. R. China.

French and African Francophone Studies Center of Hohai University

I. Introduction

The French and African Francophone Studies Center of Hohai University is a university-level specialized research institute established in October 2020, with its general office located in the College of International Languages and Cultures. It brings together experts and scholars from the College of International Languages and Cultures, the College of Water Conservancy and Hydropower Engineering, the School of Law, the Business School and others. Most of the researchers have studied or worked in France or French-speaking countries.

The center is dedicated to the studies of France and African French-speaking countries, especially those in West Africa, from the perspectives of water conservancy cooperation, food security cooperation, financial cooperation, international relations and others. The research focus of the center involves water conservancy cooperation with Africa, African food security, financial cooperation with Africa, and China-France-Africa cooperation. The center currently has 22 full-time and part-time researchers, among whom 11 have senior titles and eight have vice-senior titles.

Hohai University has fostered overseas talents for African countries at the undergraduate and postgraduate levels since the 1960s. It now offers more than 20 majors completely taught in English including hydrology and water resources, water conservancy and hydropower, migration science and management, sociology, public administration and business administration, covering the disciplines of both sciences and social sciences. Up till today, it has fostered more than 1,000 doctors, postgraduates and undergraduates. In the period beginning from 2012 alone, 1,072 African students, including 623 from the member countries of the Economic Community of West African States (ECOWAS), graduated from this university. In recent years, the number of enrollments has increased significantly, with an average of 35.24%;

Hohai University is a research and training base of hydrology and water resources of the United Nations Educational, Scientific and Cultural Organization (UNESCO) in China, and a key training base for African personnel in hydrology and water resources, water conservancy and hydropower, and migration and social security. Since the 1980s, it has conducted a large number of cooperative research and training activities with France and French-speaking countries in West Africa including Côte d'Ivoire, Guinea and Niger. In recent years, the university has worked actively with overseas universities and research institutes to establish international cooperative research centers, and participated in important projects and fields concerning with knowledge innovation. In particular, the university established Hohai-Lille College in 2020, which creates an engineer training system for French-speaking countries, makes its own contributions to China's fostering of comprehensive engineer talents with outstanding subject knowledge as well as extraordinary language skills, and allows the university to form a closed loop of scientific research, talent fostering, and discipline construction in the studies of France and French-speaking countries in Africa.

In recent years, the university has given full play to its advantages in water conservancy. Centered on the "Belt & Road Initiative" and the "Go Global" strategy, and taking the opportunity of the establishment of the regional and national research center of the Ministry of Education, it carried out scientific research, technical cooperation and training, and high-level talent fostering as to the national issues of African French-speaking countries. It also built a government-industry-university-research cooperation platform with leading companies in key industries, and undertook the tasks of research in national major and key projects and training of African hydropower engineering technicians in the field of China-Africa capacity cooperation. With first-class service and knowledge in advanced hydropower, environmental science and management science and engineering, it serves the hydropower industry and economic construction of African countries, comprehensively improves the level and ability of itself in serving the national strategy of China and hydropower development of Africa, and helps Africa improve the endogenous growth capacity, thus contributing to the establishment of a "China-Africa community with a shared future".

II. Contact Information

Contact Person: You Tao; Tel: +86-25-58099462; Email: 38500793@qq.com

Correspondence Address: Hohai University, No. 1 Xikang Road, Nanjing City, Jiangsu Province (211100), P. R. China.

Center of West African Economic Community, Hohai University

I. Introduction

The Center of West African Economic Community at Hohai University was established in March 2021, is headed by Professor Zhang Hairong, dean of the College of International Languages and Cultures of Hohai University, and brings together more than 20 experts and scholars from Hohai University specializing in science, engineering, literature and law.

The center mainly conducts research on the Economic Community of West African States (ECOWAS) as well as its member states including Benin, Burkina Faso, Togo, Cape Verde, Gambia, Guinea, Guinea-Bissau, Ghana, Côte d'Ivoire, Liberia, Mali, Niger, Nigeria, Sierra Leone and Senegal.

The main research areas of the center include: (1) major issues in West Africa: conducting comprehensive research on major issues such as water security, food supply and energy cooperation in the ECOWAS, and providing decision-making advisories for relevant national departments and institutions; (2) foreign policy of major powers toward Africa: studying the foreign affairs strategies of major powers toward Africa, exploring the profound impact of the global political pattern on the region, and building a consultancy think tank for decision-making with certain international influence and the capacity to solve major theoretical and practical problems; and (3) all-round exchanges between China and the ECOWAS: serving the need of the "Belt and Road" Initiative of China, promoting China-Africa in-depth cooperation in economic, social, cultural and other fields, carrying out all-round research on Chinese and African literature and cultural works from the comparative perspective, and enhancing the building of China's national image.

Other research areas of the center involve: (1) water, food, energy and economic issues: conducting special research on major issues such as water resource utilization, food security, energy development and ecological environment in the ECOWAS; (2) geopolitics and foreign relations: studying the important position of the ECOWAS in the political landscape of Africa and in the global architecture, and exploring the policy of major powers toward Africa and the unique role of West Africa in global development; (3) the "Belt and Road" Initiative: studying the strategic layout of Chinese enterprises in West Africa, conducting research on the trade mechanism between China and West Africa, and carrying out in-depth analysis of investment and trade risks in the ECOWAS; (4) strategies of key industries for investment in West Africa: studying the development strategies of Chinese enterprises in Africa in key areas such as hydropower, energy and transportation, and conducting comprehensive research on economic development and social governance of the ECOWAS; (5) China-Africa cultural exchanges and cooperation: carrying out translation of Chinese literature in the ECOWAS, literary exchanges between China and the member states of the ECOWAS, and research on the spreading of Chinese culture in the ECOWAS; and (6) high-level talent fostering and technical training: undertaking major projects in the field of China-Africa capacity cooperation, and promoting the training of technical personnel in the fields of water conservancy and energy for the ECOWAS.

II. Contact Information

Contact Person: You Tao; Tel: +86-25-58099462; Email: 38500793@qq.com

Correspondence Address: Hohai University, No. 1 Xikang Road, Nanjing City, Jiangsu Province (211100), P. R. China.

Côte d'Ivoire and Gulf of Guinea Research Center of Hohai University

I. Introduction

Côte d'Ivoire and Gulf of Guinea Research Center of Hohai University (CIGGRCH) was established in April 2017 , and the research center was approved as the National and Regional Research Center of the Ministry of Education in March 2021. Relying on the business school, the research center is an important measure for Hohai University to implement the "double first-class" discipline construction and promote the strategy of Chinese National Philosophy and Social Sciences 'Going Global', and will promote the output of research results. products and technologies, as well as the establishment of an international and regional government-industry-university-research cooperation platform by Countries around the Gulf of Guinea.Its establishment is also an effective exploration of the Hohai university to build an international interdisciplinary research system and a new-type high- level think tank.

By cooperating with four universities of Côte d'Ivoire and Ghana (National University of Côte d'Ivoire, Yamoussoukro National Higher Agricultural College, Bowani Institute of Technology, Nkumar University of Technology of Ghana), West Africa Alumni Association of Hohai university, China Harbour Engineering Company Ltd (CHEC), and Ghana Chinese Chamber of Commerce, the center makes efforts to build a new "1+1+1" China Africa cooperation model that integrates a training base for overseas students, a platform for academic exchanges, and a think tank of West African studies. The development objectives of the center are as follows:

A talent training base. It expands the enrollment of West African students in China,and enriches the multi-level training system for undergraduate, graduate and doctoral students. Through overseas official training, teacher training, customized training on information and communications technology (ICT) and engineering, and summer practice programs for students in West Africa, the center is striving to build a diversified overseas talent training base featuring academic education, on-the-job training and practical training.

A platform for academic research and cultural exchanges. By regularly holding international academic conferences such as the "West Africa Forum", China-Africa Friendship& Academic and Cultural Exchange Month, and promoting the China-Gulf of Guinea International Industry-University Research Cooperation Project, the center is striving to build a platform for China-Africa exchanges, cooperation and research in the fields of academic research, people-to-people exchanges, and science and technology, so as to improve the influence of Chinese universities and enterprises in Africa and enhance cultural soft power of China.

Establishing a think tank for gulf of Guinea studies. Combining with the disciplinary advantages and research characteristics of African member units, strengthening statistical, economic and social research with overseas member units of the National University of Côte d'Ivoire, and promoting cooperation and joint research with the members of west African think tank organizations such as the Policy Research Center at Nkuma University of Technology in Ghana, the center issues and undertakes research projects to provide intellectual support and decision-making consultation in key areas such as water conservancy and hydropower development, infrastructure construction and sustainable socio-economic development in Cote d 'Ivoire and the whole West Africa.

The new "1+1+1" China-Africa cooperation model in The Centre for Cote d 'Ivoire in the Gulf of Guinea studies at the Hohai university that integrates a training base for overseas students, a platform for academic exchanges, and a think tank of West African studies that can promote China's long-term and far-reaching influence on the politics, economy and trade, science and technology, humanities and education of the Gulf of Guinea countries, which could build cote d 'Ivoire and West African regional studies into a characteristic research brand of our university and form an international interdisciplinary research system with "think tank" as the guide.

The center has a Management Committee and an Advisory Committee composed of university leaders, leading academic researchers in related fields, and industry experts to guide the development direction and major decisions of the center. The center has set up one director, Professor Tian Ze, three deputy directors and one secretary: Associate professor Wu Zhaodan. Relying on the member units of the Center at home and abroad, three research labs have been established, namely, the Gulf of Guinea-Cote d 'Ivoire Economic, Trade and Investment Studies, Marine Economy, and China-Africa Cultural Studies. The Center's Cooperation and Development Department is mainly responsible for cooperation projects and business development in Guinea and West Africa. The Administration Office is responsible for day-to-day administration and financial processing.

II. Contact Information

Website: https://byoa.dataism.com.cn/a?login

Contact Person: Wu Zhaodan ; Tel: 0519-85191802; Email: 20131907@hhu.edu.cn

Correspondence Address: Room 501, Erudite Building, Business School,

211000; Hohai University, No.8 west Focheng Road, Nanjing city, Jiangsu Province, P.R.China.

Institute of African Trade and Investment, School of Economics & Management, Nanchang University

I. Introduction

The Institute of African Trade and Investment at the School of Economics & Management in Nanchang University is a non-profit organization jointly founded in May 2014 by teachers from the Department of International Economics and Trade of Nanchang University, entrepreneurs in Jiangxi Province who are concerned with African economic research, as well as banks, government consultancy institutions and laboratories related to African trade and investment.

According to the charter of the institute, its main tasks are: (1) to carry out academic research and organize academic activities; (2) to organize the application of scientific research projects at or above the provincial level; (3) to organize the application of provincial social science awards and society awards; (4) to strengthen contact with fellow universities and research institutes to promote academic exchanges; (5) to conduct exchanges and cooperation with domestic enterprises and institutions in related fields; and (6) to edit and publish internal journals featuring guidance, service and theoretical foundation. The institute extensively collects and summarizes relevant policy and environmental information on trade and investment in African countries and conducts in-depth investigations and research activities on African economy. Its main businesses are as follows: (1) conducting regular academic exchanges on African economy, organizing personnel training programs, and holding seminars on African economic development and other activities; (2) organizing experts of African studies to provide opinions and suggestions on policies of the state and various enterprises and institutions, and providing information consultancy on investment, project feasibility analysis, industry research, and market research for enterprises; and (3) completing other tasks assigned by the School of Economics & Management of Nanchang University.

The institute's research focuses on China-Africa trade and Chinese investment in Africa. By integrating government think tanks, enterprise consultancy, scientific research and teaching, it strives to build an interdisciplinary, practical and communicative platform for Nanchang University to conduct exchanges and cooperation with various disciplines and universities in terms of China-Africa trade and Chinese investment in Africa.

In addition to literature research and field research, the institute has three other research approaches. (1) The researchers give lectures for African officials in the Developing Countries Training Base in Jiangxi held by Ministry of Commerce. (2) Nearly 1,000 African undergraduate and graduate students pursue studies in the International Exchange College of Nanchang University. (3) External researchers travel between China and African countries frequently or work in Africa on a permanent basis, or their businesses have branches and offices in Africa.

At present, the institute has 15 researchers. Among them, 10 are teachers from Nanchang University, five are external researchers, five have doctoral degrees, and six hold senior professional titles. All researchers have made academic visits or conducted field research in Africa.

II. Contact Information

Contact Person: Mao Xiaoming; Tel: +86-791-83969471; Email: 805267646@qq.com

Correspondence Address: Room 406, Waijing Building, No. 999 Xuefu Avenue, Hongjiaozhou, Nanchang City, Jiangxi Province, P. R. China.

Madagascar Research Center, Jiangxi Normal University

I. Introduction

The Madagascar Research Center at Jiangxi Normal University (JXNU) was founded on June 25, 2015. Since its establishment, the center has worked in close cooperation with the "Belt and Road" Initiative and China's foreign policy to serve the formulation and implementation of the Chinese government's political and economic policies to Africa, and conducted comprehensive research on Madagascar's politics, economy, culture and society, so as to enhance mutual understanding and trust between the Chinese and Madagascan peoples and promote mutually beneficial cooperation between the two countries in various fields. JXNU has equipped the center with offices and equipments and formulated management regulations and personnel fostering programs for the center. Upon application, the center was successfully selected into the list of Regional and Country-Specific Studies Centers Registered with the Ministry of Education in July 2017. Since then, it has made efforts to complete its construction, striving to develop into a top-level research center of African country-specific studies in China with global influence as early as possible.

In September 2017, the Madagascar Research Center stopped being affliated with the Department of International Cooperation and Exchange and became an affiliate of the Foreign Languages College, thus achieving the goal of decentralization of administrative management and integration of discipline resources. Its research team comprises one director, two deputy directors, and 12 full-time and part-time researchers, including two Madagascan researchers and one secretary for scientific research. Its research covers the areas of literature, history, politics, economy, law, and folk customs of African countries, especially those of Madagascar. It teaches Chinese to the speakers of other languages in the region as well.

In May 2019, the center completed the renovation of its independent office venue. At present, it has an office, a reference room and a reception room, and plans to complete the preparatory work for the Museum of Madagascar in 2020. Up till today, it has purchased a batch of paintings, wood carvings, straw weavings, national musical instruments and ore specimens from Madagascar. When the museum is established, Madagascar art exhibition and other special exhibitions will be held to fully display the unique natural ecology and humanistic charm of Madagascar and Africa at large.

In recent years, the center has formulated regulations to encourage its researchers to apply for projects, publish academic papers, and write research monographs. By 2019, the center has completed two special projects of the Ministry of Education, namely, Research on Trade Policy of Madagascar and Research on Ethnic Policy of Madagascar. It has completed four self-funded public bidding projects, including Research on China's Foreign Policy Towards Madagascar, Study of Madagascar's Educational Changes, China's New Aid Policy to Africa: A Case Study of Madagascar's Modernization, and Study of Madagascar's Geopolitics in the 19th Century. In 2018, the center completed Madagascar Education Report required by the Ministry of Education. Its researchers published 13 papers on studies of Madagascar and Africa at large. It completed the validation and proofreading of three books of Madagascar Studies Series, including *Concise Madagascar Language*, *Slang Collection of Madagascar Language* and *Folk Tales of Madagascar*, which will soon be published. Recently, preparations are being made for the publication of *2019 Annual Journal of Madagascar Studies* and *Selected Works of French Literature in Madagascar Studies*. The center plans to publish three book of the series every year, striving to build the series as the publications with large scale and great influence in the field of African studies in China within three years. In addition, the center is working on the translation of *Madagascar Law* in preparation for the participation in the translation of African law collections by the China-Africa Institute.

Researchers of the center have actively participated in academic exchanges of regional and country-specific studies at home and abroad in various ways. Led by the director, the researchers have visited the Institute of African Studies at Zhejiang Normal University, the China-ASEAN Research Institute of Guangxi University, and the Center for African Studies at Peking University for exchanges and learning. Meanwhile, they have actively participated in various academic conferences organized by administrative authorities and fellow universities to guide and promote the establishment and development of the center's academic research. In addition, since its inception, the center has continuously invited domestic and international experts and scholars to give academic lectures. Researchers of the center have also carried out field research in Madagascar to obtain first-hand research data.

In order to strengthen disciplinary construction and personnel fostering, the center integrated its resources and helped the Foreign Languages College apply for the Level-2 master program of French Language and Literature in October 2019. The master's program was officially approved in November 2019 and students will be enrolled in September 2020. African Regional and Country-Specific Studies will be listed as a course in the program. In 2020, the Foreign Languages College applied for the Level-1 doctoral program of Foreign Languages and Literature and listed African regional and country-specific studies as one of its four directions.

II. Contact Information

Website: http://mrc.jxnu.edu.cn/

Contact Person: Chen Lijuan; Tel: +86-791-88120324; Email: 804412178@qq.com

Correspondence Address: Yaohu Campus, Jiangxi Normal University, No. 99 Ziyang Avenue, Nanchang City, Jiangxi Province (330022), P. R. China.

Tunisia Studies Center, Dalian University of Foreign Languages

I. Introduction

The Tunisia Studies Center at Dalian University of Foreign Languages (DLUFL) was established in 2007 and is now a Regional and Country-Specific Studies Center Registered with the Ministry of Education focusing on the studies of politics, economy, history, culture and international relations of Tunisia.

The center will, relying on the platform of friendly cooperation between DLUFL and the Carthage University Tunis, and by virtue of good research strength and language advantages of DLUFL, work actively to build a regional and country-specific research base focusing on Tunisia, make efforts to develop a research team with strong research abilities and great influence, continuously improve the quality of research, and strive to develop into a research center with professional advantages and significant impact, providing consultancy services for government departments and foreign-related enterprises.

The center will monitor political developments around Tunisia over the next five years; provide policy advisories on major practical issues including China-Tunisia relations and the national situation of Tunisia; strengthen its capacity in offering practical solutions, predicting the situational development and providing quick response advisories; guide the public opinion; promote think-tank diplomacy; and make efforts to develop into a bridge and link between China and Tunisia for the development of the bilateral friendship.

The center adheres to the principle of "focusing on major issues and serving national strategies", and focuses on the studies of "contemporary and modern development of Tunisian political culture" and "status quo of Chinese language learning in Tunisia and its learning and service needs in the future".

In 2015, the center organized the first national academic seminar on "Tunisian Issues and Islamic Culture in the Arab World". Attending the seminar were nearly 30 leaders, distinguished guests, experts and scholars including Ambassador Yang Fuchang, former vice foreign minister; Professor Zhang Hong, doctoral advisor of Beijing Foreign Studies University; and Li Yuanqing, vice president of the China-Arab Exchange Association. In January 2017, at the invitation of Ambassador Dhia Khaled of Tunisia to China, President Liu Hong of DLUFL paid a visit to the Ambassador at the Tunisian Embassy in Beijing. The two sides exchanged in-depth views on educational and cultural cooperation between DLUFL and Tunisia, the establishment of a Confucius Institute at the Carthage University Tunis, the development of the Tunisia Studies Center at DLUFL, and others. In September 2017, Professor Mohamed Khalil, president of the Morocco-China Friendship and Exchange Association, visited the Tunis Studies Center and held a meeting with Vice President Jiang Fengchun of DLUFL and the heads of relevant departments including the International Exchange Office and the Department of Italian and Arabic Studies. The two sides exchanged views on strengthening exchanges of teachers and students between Chinese and Moroccan universities and setting up research platforms, and held in-depth talks on enhancing the development of friendly relations between China and Morocco and promoting cooperation between China and North Africa in the fields of education, economy, trade and culture. In 2019, the researchers of the center gained the approval of one youth project of the Ministry of Education and one project of the Center for Language Education and Cooperation, and published a translated monograph of more than 200,000 words. In early July 2020, the center submitted materials for its assessment, summarized its work in the past five years and made better planning for the future work.

In the future, the Tunis Studies Center will keep focusing on Tunisian studies and gradually expand its research to North African countries, or even all African countries, thus forming a research scope centering around Tunisia, covering North Africa, and extending to the whole Africa, so as to constantly make new and greater contributions to the "Belt and Road" initiative as well as national and local economic and social development.

II. Contact Information

Contact Person: Zhang Jingshu; Tel: +86-411-86111078; Email: zhangjingshu@dlufl.edu.cn

Website: https://tunsc.dlufl.edu.cn/

Correspondence Address: Room 7A507, School of Asian and African Studies, Dalian University of Foreign Languages, No. 6 West Section of Lvshun South Road, Lvshunkou District, Dalian City, Liaoning Province (730070), P. R. China.

China-Africa Trade Research Center

I. Introduction

Founded in June 2014 and affiliated with Afrindex.com, the China-Africa Trade

Research Center is a professional China-Africa trade think tank, specializing in research on dozens of industries, particulary on seven major industries including electromechanical equipment, food, medicine, textile, new energy, building materials and chemical industry.

The center is based on 54 African countries, and mainly focuses on African subdivided industries, including the research on the current situation of African industrial development and the prediction of development trends, to meet the demands of Chinese enterprises for in-depth industrial cognition and business strategy formulation in Africa. In the year 2019 alone, the center wrote eight African general market analysis reports, including African Automobile Market Analysis Report, African Textile-Printing and Dyeing Market Analysis Report, African Paint Market Analysis Report, African Household Appliance Market Analysis Report, African Refrigerator Market Analysis Report, African Oil and Gas Refining Market Analysis Report, Report on Investment in Infrastructure Industries in Africa, and African Polyurethane Foam Market Analysis Report.

Since its establishment, the China-Africa Trade Research Center has compiled more than 1,000 analysis reports of general markets for seven major industries in Africa and hundreds of customized in-depth market analysis reports for enterprises. It aspires to develop into China's largest private think tank for African industrial research.

In terms of personnel fostering, the center follows the philosophy of "industry-university-research" integration in talent fostering; carries out in-depth cooperation with key domestic universities such as Southwest Jiaotong University, the Center for West African Studies at the University of Electronic Science and Technology of China, and Southwestern University of Finance and Economics; and works actively to build a mature development system of "University-Enterprise Alliance" to promote students' all-round development including theories at class, field investigations, and enterprise practice. Up till today, the center has helped more than 10 African doctoral students settle in the operation centers of Afrindex.com in African countries to practice market research and operation.

II. Contact Information

Website: http://news.afrindex.com/

WeChat Official Account: afrindex

Contact Person: Li Min; Email: jessica@af-can.cn

Correspondence Address: Level 13, Building A, China Overseas International Center, No. 177 Jiaozi Avenue, Gaoxin District, Chengdu City, Sichuan Province, P. R. China.

Center for African Studies, Southwestern University of Finance and Economics

I. Introduction

Founded in 2016, the Center for African Studies at Southwestern University of Finance and Economics is the university's first National and Regional Studies Center Registered with the Ministry of Education. It boasts profound academic achievements and extensive experience in foreign cooperation. Its research team includes a number of scholars with overseas research experience and doctoral degrees from world-renowned universities, as well as former commercial counsellors of Chinese embassies and experts in the fields of international tax and merger and acquisition from famous accounting firms. Professor Dong Yan is the director.

In response to the "Belt and Road" Initiative, the center conducts in-depth research on the opportunities and risks of Chinese enterprises investing in African countries. It has complete hardware facilities and abundant electronic information resources, including dozens of databases and data terminals such as ScienceDirect, Springer, Bloomberg and Wind. Its main work includes fundamental research, applied research, consultancy services, early warning of risks, and education of international students. Under the framework of "international production capacity cooperation", it is committed to providing effective policy suggestions for Chinese enterprises to give full play to their comparative advantages, carry out strategic transfer and transformation, and achieve "win-win" or even "multi-win" economic cooperation between China and foreign countries. It also provides high-quality research and consultancy services to the government and transnational companies on China-Africa economy and finance.

The scientific research achievements of the center since its establishment are as follows: (1) It has completed four regional and country-specific studies projects commissioned by the Ministry of Education. They are "Research on Kenya's Policy on Financial Risk", "International Cooperation in the Development of African High-tech Industries and China's Cooperation Strategies", "Handbook on Angola Education" and "Handbook on Zimbabwe Education". (2) It has collected detailed data on China's investment in African countries since 2003, including the detailed information about more than 4,000 investment projects. It has systematically studied the impact factors on investment risks and financial risks in Africa, such as industrial chain transfer, environmental regulation, corruption, and economic policies, and published multiple academic papers on the study of China-Africa trade cooperation relations and the impact of environmental regulation on China-Africa investment. (3) The center has established the "Investment Information Platform for Major African Countries and Cities" and regularly publishes information of investment risks of target countries and the latest information on related investment projects in Africa, providing valuable decision-making reference for Chinese investors. The data source of the platform is mainly a data collection system based on local information channels. The center has organized more than 10 African students to regularly carry out "Surveys of Investment Environment in Major African Cities", collecting data on the prices of daily necessities, asset prices, exchange rate, social security, political stability and infrastructure every one or two months. Up till today, they have covered five countries and eight cities in Africa. (4) It has created a visual transportation database to collect informaion of transportation routes and trade duration between Chinese provinces and major African cities. (5) In June 2018, it hosted economic and trade cooperation forum based on the discipline advantages of the Research

Institute of Economics and Management. Actively responding to the "Belt and Road" Initiative, it expands the exchange fields, transmits advanced academic ideas, and shares academic achievements with experts and scholars around the world. The center hosted the Cross Country Perspectives in Finance (CCPF) Conferences in Dar es Salaam, Tanzania in December 2018 and Mauritius in 2019, inviting scholars from world-renowned universities to jointly discuss the risks of cross-border investment in the current complex financial environment. In addition, they visited Chinese government offices and a number of Chinese-funded enterprises during the conferences.

In the past four-odd years since its establishment, the center has made great achievements in international cooperation and exchanges, bringing a good external environment to its development. Meanwhile, its long-term fundamental research has gradually yielded a number of valuable achievements in terms of academic research and foreign services. The progress in fundamental research should be credited to the resources of African students in the university. These students are familiar with their own national conditions and can effectively contribute to the investigation and research. The center encouraged the African students to participate in the "Survey of Investment Environment in Major African Countries and Cities" and provided learning and practicing opportunities for them in survey formulation, questionnaire design, survey implementation, and data collation and analysis. Up to December 2019, with the support of the Center for African Studies and the Research Institute of Economics and Management, the Southwestern University of Finance and Economics has successively reached agreement with the University of Gondar of Ethiopia, Wolkite University of Ethiopia, and the College of Business Education of Tanzania on the training of African teachers. Now these projects are already in the stage of contract signing and implementation.

The future objectives of the center are as follows: Firstly, the center will further optimize disciplinary construction and personnel fostering, further systematize the relevant framework, and enrich the curriculum. Secondly, it will strive to enhance its consultancy capabilities for decision-making, intensify its consultancy services for the government, and promote the progress of consultancy services and academic research. Thirdly, now that the "Investment Information Platform for Major African Countries and Cities" has been initially established and has released relevant investment reference information to enterprises, the key work will be to further enrich the information content and regularly release the "Investment Risk Assessment Report" of specific countries.

II. Contact Information

Website: http://riem.swufe.edu.cn/

Contact Person: Yu Kexin; Tel: +86-28-87098241; Email: yukexincd@163.com

Correspondence Address: Room 1214, Gezhi Building, Southwestern University of Finance and Economics, No. 555 Liutai Avenue, Chengdu City, Sichuan Province, P. R. China.

Center for West African Studies, University of Electronic Science and Technology of China

I. Introduction

The Center for West African Studies at the University of Electronic Science and Technology of China (UESTC) was established in April 2017 on the basis of the School of Public Affairs and Administration of the UESTC. Its establishment is an important measure for promoting the strategy of Chinese National Philosophy and Social Sciences 'Going Global', and will promote the output of research results, products and technologies, as well as the establishment of an international and regional government-industry-university-research cooperation platform by West African countries. Its establishment is also an effective exploration of the UESTC to build an international interdisciplinary research system and a new-type high-level think tank.

By cooperating with five universities of Ghana (the University of Ghana, the University of Education, the University of Cape Coast of Ghana, the University for Development Studies, and the Ghana Institute of Management and Public

Administration), West Africa Alumni Association of UESTC, and Ghana Chinese Chamber of Commerce, the center makes efforts to build a new "1+1+1" China-Africa cooperation model that integrates a training base for overseas students, a platform for academic exchanges, and a think tank of West African studies. (1) A talent training base. It expands the enrollment of West African students in China, and enriches the multi-level training system for undergraduate, graduate and doctoral students. Through overseas official training, teacher training, customized training on information and communications technology (ICT) and engineering, and summer practice programs for students in West Africa, the center is striving to build a diversified overseas talent training base featuring academic education, on-the-job training and practical training. (2) A platform for academic research and cultural exchanges. By regularly holding international academic conferences such as the "West Africa Forum" and the China-Africa Friendship & Academic and Cultural Exchange Month, and promoting the 3D platform of cultural resources and the China-West Africa International Industry-University-Research Cooperation Project, the center is striving to build a platform for China-Africa exchanges, cooperation and research in the fields of academic research, people-to-people exchanges, and science and technology, so as to improve the influence of Chinese universities and enterprises in Africa and enhance cultural soft power of China. (3) A think tank for West African studies. The center publishes and undertakes research projects to provide policy advisory for the Chinese government and West African countries on the basis of combining the discipline advantages and studies of African member units and strengthening cooperation and joint research with overseas member organizations such as the Institute of Statistics, Social and Economic Research of the University of Ghana (ranking 164th among global think tanks), Imani Center for Policy & Education of Ghana (ranking 113th among global think tanks), and West African think tank organizations such as the African School of Economics and the Laboratory of Studies and Research on Social Dynamics and Local Development (LASDEL) of Benin.

The new "1+1+1" China-Africa cooperation model of the center that integrates a training base for overseas students, a platform for academic exchanges, and a think tank of West African studies can promote China's long-term and far-reaching influence on West Africa in the fields of politics, trade and economy, science and technology, people-to-people exchanges, and education; and strengthen the study of international, regional and country-specific issues, which will help to fill the gap in West African studies in China and form an international interdisciplinary research system oriented toward "think tanks".

The center has a Management Committee and an Advisory Committee, which are composed of relevant university leaders, leading academic researchers in relevant fields, and industry experts, who guide the development direction and make major decisions for the center. The center has one director and four deputy directors. Under the center are two institutes, namely, the Institute of West African Social Governance and the Institute for China-African Humanistic Studies based on the member units at home and abroad. Besides, the center has a Cooperative Development Department governing the cooperation projects and business development in West Africa and an Administrative Office responsible for daily administration and financial work. In 2019, the center invited Mr. Li Anshan, professor of the School of International Studies of Peking University and chairman of the Chinese Society of African Historical Studies, to be a contract professor of the UESTC, and Dr. Guillaume Moumouni (Benin) of the University of Abomey-Calavi of Benin and the School of International Studies of Peking University to be an assistant researcher of the center.

The short-term goal of the center is to become a guiding unit of the "China-Africa Joint Research and Exchange Program" of the Ministry of Foreign Affairs and the Chinese think tank unit of the "China-Africa Think Tanks 10+10 Partnership Plan". Its medium-term goal is to be selected into the list of Regional and Country-Specific Studies Centers Registered with the Ministry of Education. The long-term goal is to build a think tank of West African studies with global influence.

II. Contact Information

Website: http://cwas.uestc.edu.cn/indexZh.html/

WeChat Official Account: gh_bfde9ecc926a

Contact Person: Zhang Mengmeng (Executive); Fax: +86-28-61831756; Email: zhangmengmeng2013@163.com

Correspondence Address: Qingshuihe Campus, University of Electronic Science and Technology of China, No. 2006 Xiyuan Avenue,West Hi-Tech Zone, Chengdu City, Sichuan Province, P. R. China.

Center for Ethiopian Studies, China West Normal University

I. Introduction

The Center for Ethiopian Studies is a substantive research institution managed by China West Normal University. It was prepared in early 2017 and was formally established in June 2017. To meet the needs of the "Belt and Road" Initiative, the center aims to enhance China's social and cultural understanding of Ethiopia and related regions through integrating the university's resources of research on Ethiopian, African issues and African Americans. By conducting interdisciplinary research on Ethiopia and its neighboring countries in various domains, the center promotes disciplinary construction and academic research of the university, provides intellectual support for relevant decision-making of the government and businesses, and builds a platform for academic exchanges and economic cooperation between Sichuan Province and Ethiopia, so as to enhance friendship between China and Ethiopia. The center focuses on politics, diplomacy, economy, literature, culture, history, religion and ethnic issues of Ethiopia, as well as interaction between Ethiopia and its neighboring countries and major countries outside the region. It pays special attention to political and diplomatic relations, English literature, ethnic and religious issues, history and culture, economic development, and national modernization of Ethiopia. Currently, the center has 11 members, including one part-time researcher. Among them there are nine professors and associate professors, one lecturer and one teaching assistant.

Since its preparation period, the center has carried out multiple academic activities and published two academic works. During its preparation, the academic lecture entitled "The Belt and Road Initiative: Implementation of Theoretical Innovation of China's Diplomatic Practice in the New Era" was held in the Academic Hall of Chaoyang Building, Huafeng Campus. The lecture was hosted by China West Normal University and jointly organized by the Scientific Research Office and the School of Foreign Languages. Mr. Ai Ping, member of the Chinese People's Political Consultative Conference (CPPCC), former Chinese ambassador to Ethiopia, former vice minister of the International Department of the CCCPC, and vice president of the Chinese Association for International Understanding, gave the lecture. On November 11, 2017, the "Translation Conference & the Belt and Road Initiative Translation Symposium" was held in the Academic Hall of Beihu Campus of China West Normal University with the Translators Association of Sichuan as the host and the Center for Ethiopian Studies as the co-organizer. Researchers of the center participated in the thematic forum of "Translation and Translation Studies Under the Background of the Belt and Road Initiative" and held group discussions on the prospect of translation studies in China and Africa. In January 2018, the article "Ethiopia Will Become a Global Manufacturing Center" written by Mr. Shen Shiwei, a part-time researcher at the center and professor of China Foreign Affairs University, was published in *Global Times*. In June 2018, Professor ShenShiwei published the article "Building a Community with a Shared Future for China and Africa" in *Guangming Daily*. On June 29, 2018, Professor Xia Yanhua, director of the center, and several other researchers attended the academic conference on "Development Prospects of China-India Relations after Wuhan Summit" hosted by China West Normal University.

The long-term development goal of the center is to build a base of Ethiopian studies with distinctive features and comprehensive research fields. It plans to establish an influential website and an important publication on Ethiopian studies, undertake national projects independently, and provide relevant information on

Ethiopia for the government and enterprises.

II. Contact Information

Website: http://scasobyzx.jwz500.com/

Contact Person: Xia Yanhua; Email: 1229326835@qq.com

Correspondence Address: School of Foreign Languages, China West Normal University, No. 1 Shida Road, Shunqing District, Nanchong City, Sichuan Province, P. R. China.

Center for African Studies, University of Jinan

I. Introduction

In order to implement the directive of the Ministry of Education in 2012 that regional and country-specific studies should "gradually expand the coverage of target countries", the University of Jinan enhanced policy guidance, provied project support and strengthened mechanism development, and established the Research Center for Francophone Countries of Africa in 2014, with Professor Fan Yuejin, former party secretary of the university, as the director. In 2017, the center was selected into the list of Regional and Country-Specific Studies Centers Registered with the Ministry of Education, with the name changed into the Center for African Studies at the University of Jinan. Professor Li Changlei, dean of the School of Foreign Languages of the university, is the incumbent director and Mr. Li Zhaoxing, former Chinese foreign minister, is the honorary director. At present, the center has 33 full-time and part-time members, including three senior diplomats, 17 professors, eight associate professors, three lecturers and two foreign experts.

Relying on the advantages of the University of Jinan as a comprehensive university with a variety of disciplines and taking the School of Foreign Languages as the carrier, the center actively integrates academic advantages of the School of International Education and Exchange, the School of Resources and Environment, the School of Liberal Arts, the Business School, the School of Political Science and Law, and the School of History and Culture Industry, and absorbs the research strength outside the university, making full use of academic resources and platforms of relevant units inside and outside the university to carry out research on Africa. On August 10, 2019, the Center for African Studies at the University of Jinan was approved as the think tank for foreign affairs research and development in Shandong Province, and since then has provided strong support for the open and scientific decision-making related to foreign affairs in Shandong Province.

The center has three main research fields. (1) Research on Francophone countries of Africa and the Congo River Basin countries. Taking the Republic of the Congo as the initial research focus, the center gradually expands research to all Francophone countries of Africa, especially the countries in the Congo River Basin, covering the areas of economy, politics, history, culture, education, literature and art, foreign relations, and ecological environment. (2) Research on water resources and environment in Africa. The center mainly focuses on the management and sustainable utilization of water resources in African countries, the impact of mining on water resources and ecosystems, the impact of coalbed methane and shale gas on groundwater, the exploration and development of groundwater resources, cross-border water resources issues and policies, and the impact of climate change on regional drought and floods. Taking the advantage of the University of Jinan being the core unit of the China-Africa Water Forum, the center sent out multiple researchers to attend the forum, making the voice of Chinese scholars heard in international academic forums. (3) Research on China-Africa cultural exchanges. The center mainly conducts research in the fields of languages, literature, music, and fine arts of African countries, and actively carries out research on the promotion of Chinese culture in Africa based on the Confucius Institute jointly established by the University of Jinan and Marien Ngouabi University of the Republic of the Congo.

The specific research plans of the center are as follows: (1) Studies on society and culture. The center will study the political systems and political parties of African countries, and clarify the development of the political systems, including existing parties, their purposes, forces and relations among them; study the laws of African countries in the aspects of commerce, investment and labor; study the population, nationality, relations among ethnic groups and customs of African countries; and study African literature, history, philosophy, education, sports, art, folk proverbs and others. (2) Studies on economy and cooperation. The center will study and summarize the monetary and financial situation of African countries, including their monetary and financial cooperation with Britain, France, America and other countries; and study and summarize the current economic situation, industrial structure, economic reform of African countries, China-Africa economic cooperation experience, and the development patterns of African countries. (3) Studies on resources and environment. Through cooperation with relevant institutions in African countries, the center will carry out field investigations about local water resources, mineral resources, soil, atmosphere, ecological protection and provide practical suggestions for ecological protection in Africa. (4) Studies on China-Africa relations. The center will study the history, current situation and developing trend of China-Africa diplomatic relations and cooperation in the fields of medical care, culture, education and sports, making contributes to China-Africa exchanges and cooperation. (5) Studies on the promotion of Chinese culture. Based on Confucius Institutes, Chinese Cultural Centers and mass media, the center will study and summarize the experience and shortcomings in promoting Chinese language and culture in Africa.

Since its establishment, the center has completed works, research reports and investigation reports such as *Studies on Francophone Countries of Africa*, *Tales and Legends of Africa (French-Chinese)*, *Handbook on Education of the Republic of the Congo* and *Studies on the Relationship between China and the Republic of the Congo*.

II. Contact Information

Contact Person: Li Changlei; Tel: +86-531-82765846; Email: sfl_tr@ujn.edu.cn

Correspondence Address: School of Foreign Languages, University of Jinan, No. 336 Nanxinzhuang West Road, Shizhong District, Jinan City, Shandong Province (250022), P. R. China.

Africa Research Center, Northwest A&F University

I. Introduction

Established in June 2017, the Africa Relation Center of Northwest A&F University is a Regional and Country-Specific Studies Center Registered with the Ministry of Education.

The center takes Mauritius, Lesotho, Liberia, Libya, Morocco and Malawi as main research objects, but is not limited to these African countries. Its main research areas include agricultural resource assessment and resource information management in Africa, policies for the protection, development and utilization of agricultural resources (especially agricultural species resources) in Africa, resource strategies and development priorities of developed countries and new economies in Africa, agricultural resource development and utilization and economic and trade cooperation in Africa, and agricultural development and poverty reduction approaches in Africa.

The center has completed the Research on Early Warning Mechanisms and Adaptive Technologies in African Arid Regions, a project of the China-UN Water Action in Africa, the research on drought-resistant variety selection and breeding and cultivation technology system of maize in Egypt, the project of drought-resistant variety selection and breeding technology and variety demonstration, the project of cooperation, exploration and demonstration of water-saving agriculture technology in drylands in Africa, and the research on agricultural science and technology development strategies of Egypt.

The center recruits African students and has fostered five undergraduates in Agronomy and 35 graduates and doctoral students. These African students have made great contributions in agricultural management and scientific research departments in different countries. The center has sent eight volunteers and graduate students to African countries for exchanges, which greatly promotes the internationalization of the domestic agricultural business. In addition, the center has undertaken 30 African nations' visit projects of the Foreign

Economic Cooperation Center of the Ministry of Agriculture and Rural Affairs, the Department of International Trade and Economic Affairs of the Ministry of Commerce, the Department of Agriculture and Rural Affairs of Shaanxi Province, Shaanxi Provincial Department of Commerce, and the Bureau of International Cooperation of Yangling Agricultural Hi-tech Industrial Demonstration Zone, and conducted 48 special training sessions for over 900 participants.

The center completed the technology assistance tasks of China-aided Agro-technology Demonstration Centers in Benin and Cameroon. The center finished the feasibility study for a number of projects, including the Agro-technology Demonstration Center in Cameroon of Shaanxi NK Group and Shaanxi Overseas Investment and Development Co, Ltd, the Vanilla Industry Development in Comorin of China New Era International Engineering Corporation, the farm project in Djibouti of Yangling Hanhan Egg Product Co, Ltd, and the 10,000-head cattle farm project in Côte d'Ivoire of the International Engineering Department of Shaanjian Group. It also conducted agricultural project assessment and evaluation in Tanzania, Zimbabwe and Cameroon.

Since its establishment, the center has obtained a series of achievements on policy advisory, including the Operation Plan of China-aided Agro-technology Demonstration Center in Cameroon, the Comorian Vanilla Industry Development Research Report, the Zimbabwe Agricultural Region Planning Report, the Technology Program of China-aided Agro-technology Demonstration Center in Tanzania, the Egyptian Agricultural Science and Technology Development Report, the Training Program of China-aided Agro-technology Demonstration Center in Benin, and the Study Report of the Farming System in the Nile Delta of Egypt.

The center strives to develop into a think tank for African agricultural policy-making, a technical platform for the exploration, development and utilization of African resources, an academic center on African agricultural economy, society, culture and history, a base for fostering high-level talents engaged in fundamental and applied research on Africa, and a bridge for China-Africa economic and trade cooperation and transformation of science and technology.

The center currently has eight full-time researchers and four part-time experts. Professor HaiJiangbo acts as the director.

II. Contact Information

Website: https://arc.nwsuaf.edu.cn/

WeChat Official Account: gh_00c2d30f4d0c

Contact Person: Guo Yong; Tel: +86-29-87082311; Email: 634081078@qq.com

Correspondence Address: Room 924, Africa Relation Center, Northwest A&F University, No. 3 Taicheng Road, Yangling, Xianyang City, Shaanxi Province, P. R. China.

African Studies Center of Northwest University

I. Introduction

On September 3, 2018, in his speech at the opening ceremony of the 2018 Beijing Summit of the Forum on China-Africa Cooperation, President Xi Jinping proposed to focus on the implementation of the "Eight Major Initiatives" in collaboration with African countries, and announced that "China decides to establish an institute of African studies to enhance exchanges with Africa on civilization". Based on this, the Chinese Academy of Social Sciences established the China-Africa Institute and founded the *Journal of China-Africa Studies*, which signifies that China has increased its research efforts and attention to Africa. Under the background of "profound changes unseen in a century" and the intensified strategic game between China and the United States, African studies has become increasingly important. The Northwest University enjoys long-standing advantages in the national and regional research, and has led the research in China in the fields of the Middle East history, the North African history, the Central Asian history and the South Asian history. To actively respond to the country's strategic needs, further integrate resources of relevant disciplines in regional and national studies, and promote sustainable development of related disciplines including foreign language and literature and world history, the Northwest

University officially established the African Studies Center on December 25, 2020.

The center adheres to the tenet of "satisfying actual needs based on fundamental research". Relying on the university's disciplinary advantages in West Asian and North African studies, under the interdisciplinary, integrative and cross-referential concept of the New Liberal Arts, and integrating resources of different disciplines, the center specializes in the studies of African political and economic development; African history, culture and religion; African exchanges with other countries and regions; African international organizations, China-Africa cooperation and Shaanxi-Africa cooperation. By recruiting first-class talents in the whole country, the center aims to develop into a key academic research platform, policy advisory agency, and international exchange and cooperation base in the field of African studies in middle and western China.

The Institute of Middle Eastern Studies at the Northwest University has a group of nearly 10 people specializing in North African research. They have made noticeable achievements in the field, including the eight-volume *General History of the Arab States in Africa* published in 2020 on the basis of the National Social Science Fund of China, which is the first domestic work in relevant fields. The School of Foreign Languages boasts a large faculty team with a high ratio of young teachers and highly-educated teachers as well as a high level of internationalization and academic extension, which indicates potential in conducting further African studies. The Institute of Middle Eastern Studies, the History School, the Institute of Silk Road Studies, and the Syrian Research Center have all conducted in-depth cooperation with the School of Foreign Languages in national and regional research, such as jointly fostering undergraduates majoring in world history and recruiting young teachers from the School of Foreign Languages to study for doctoral degrees. In addition, as the vice-director unit of the Asian and African Studies Society of China, the university has kept close ties with top domestic African studies institutes including the China-Africa Institute, the Institute of West-Asian and African Studies at the Chinese Academy of Social Sciences, the Center for African Studies at Peking University, and the Institute of

African Studies at Zhejiang Normal University. The leaders of the China-Africa Institute have expressed high expectations for the establishment of the center in the university and in-depth cooperation with the center in the future.

The center aims to (1) build a well-known African research platform in middle and western China: pooling together outstanding talents from within and outside the university and from home and abroad, study major theories, strategies and policies related to African development and China-Africa cooperation from new perspectives, in new approaches, and with new mechanisms, form characteristics of African studies of the Northwest University in several aspects in five to ten years, and strive to develop into a first-class research platform in this field in middle and western China; (2) develop a first-class think tank in African studies: compile a book series of *Entering Africa* and regularly release a briefing of *Latest Information of Africa* to provide references regarding China-Africa cooperation and Shaanxi-Africa cooperation for enterprises having a strong desire to develop in Africa as well as institutes and scholars engaged in African studies; (3) gain the high ground in fostering talents of African studies: foster high-level interdisciplinary talents in the fields of African development, China-Africa cooperation and African history studies, build a high-level research group with a reasonable structure, and closely integrate research results with new curriculum development so as to promote the reform in the teaching content of regional and national studies; and (4) promote the establishment of a China-Africa International Exchange and Cooperation Center: establish contacts with African universities, send scholars and students to each other, carry out exchanges and academic visits, seek cooperation in domestic and foreign projects, and hold academic forums and seminars regularly or irregularly.

The center is a non-physical institute and is affiliated to the School of Foreign Languages at the Northwest University. It has one director, one deputy director and one secretary. The director is responsible for organization, planning, coordination and implementation of research projects. The deputy director is responsible for daily management, teaching, executive administration, external liaison and coordination. The secretary assists in various tasks of the institute. The center currently has 10 researchers, all of whom have doctoral degrees. Among them are five professors, three associate professors and two lecturers. The research covers the fields of West Asia and North Africa, relations between Africa and major powers, Maghrib, and African international organizations.

II. Contact Information

Contact Person: Wang Guodong; Tel: +86-29-88308158; Email: wgd@nwu.edu.cn

Correspondence Address: School of Foreign Languages, Northwest University, No. 1 Xuefu Avenue, Chang'an District, Xi'an City, Shaanxi Province (710127), P. R. China.

The African Studies Center of Xi 'an International Studies University

I. Introduction

The African Studies Center of Xi'an International Studies University was established in April 2021. In December 2020, Xi'an International Studies University and China-Africa Institute signed a long-term strategic cooperation agreement. The two sides agreed to give full play to their disciplinary advantages and carry out close cooperation in academic researches, academic exchanges, and joint personnel training, so as to contribute to promoting China-Africa pragmatic cooperation.

The African Studies Center is attached to the School of Asian and African Studies, Xi'an International Studies University. The school currently opens 11 language majors, including Arabic, Swahili and so forth, covering a vast range of regions, including Northeast Asia, Southeast Asia, South Asia, Middle East and Africa. It is a major base in western China for the training of non-universal foreign language talents and the conducting of scientific researches concerning a wide scope of foreign languages. At present, the center has 16 part-time researchers, 12 of whom enjoy senior professional titles. Prof. Ma Fude, Dean of the School of

Asian and African Studies, is the director of the research center.

The African Studies Center of Xi'an International Studies University focuses on the overall situation of national development and China-Africa cooperation, combines the advantages of languages and other disciplines of Xi'an International Studies University, carries out the construction of African local knowledge, pays attention to the academic translation and research between China and Africa while also concentrating on the development practice of contemporary China-Africa relations, and explores the epochal significance of China-Africa exchanges under the context of global dialogue between civilizations.

II. Contact Information

Contact: Yang Ruhai; Contact number: 85319141; Email: dyxy@xisu.edu.cn

Mailing address: African Studies Center, Xi’an International Studies University, No.1 South Wenyuan Road, Guodu Educational and Technological Industry Development Zone, Chang’an District, Xi'an; Post Code: 710128

Institute of African Studies, East China Normal University

I. Introduction

The Institute of African Studies at the East China Normal University (ECNU), formerly known as the African History Research Office of the Department of History of the ECNU, was founded in 1985. The first director of the research office was Professor Ai Zhouchang, who was succeeded by Mu Tao in 1996. In June 2010, with the approval of the university, the Center for African Studies of the ECNU was established with the research office as the main body, and was affiliated to the Department of History. In May 2011, the center was renamed the Institute of African Studies, and the ECNU-UDSM (University of Dar es Salaam) Tanzania Joint Research Center was established and affiliated to the institute. The inauguration ceremony was held when the president of the UDSM visited the university in the same year. On December 5, 2018, in order to promote African research and deepen the cooperation between the two unniversities, the UDSM-

ECNU Workstation was officially established.

Taking advantage of the comprehensive disciplines of the ECNU, the institute conducts African fundamental research and talent fostering, embraces both arts and sciences, and focuses its research in the following three areas: First, based on the Tanzania Joint Research Center and the "China-Africa Universities 20+20 Cooperation Plan" of the Ministry of Education, it focuses on African history and culture studies, especially studies on East African history and culture and relations between China and Africa. Second, by virtue of the advantage in the international comparative education research of the ECNU, it conducts studies on African education. Third, the State Key Laboratory of Estuarine and Coastal Research of the ECNU and the Marine Science Institute of the UDSM work together to conduct research in East Africa on sediment deposition and erosion dynamics of estuaries and coasts under the influence of natural and human activities, the biogeochemical processes of mangrove ecosystems, and the ecological structure and function of off-shore waters in response to eutrophication.

The center now has seven researchers, including four professors, one associate professor and three lecturers. They all come from the Department of History, the School of Advanced International and Area Studies, the Faculty of Education, and the Institute for Estuarine and Coastal Science Research of the ECNU. The center also has eight external part-time professors and more than 10,000 volumes of books and reference materials on African history and culture.

The important publications published by the institute include: *History of Early Colonial Invasion* (People's Publishing House, 1982), *Selected Works of History of China-Africa Relations (1500-1918)* (1989), *Africa* (three-volume edition) (1955), *History of China-Africa Relations* (1996), *Africa Black Civilization* (1999), *Studies on South AfricaModernization* (2000), *The Republic of South Africa—In the Clashes of Black Culture and White Culture* (2000), *Modernization Studies on Countries and Regions in Asia and Africa* (2009), *African Black Wisdom (2000), Studies on Foreign Relations of South Africa* (2003), *History of Nigeria* (Translation, 2010), *Guide to World States: Burkina Faso and Togo* (Social Science Academic Press, 2011), *President Y.K. Museveni and Uganda* (2013), *The Selected Works of Julius Kambarage Nyerere* (4 volumes) (Translation, 2014), and *Historical Manuscripts of Ancient Sino-African Relations* (2019). The institute has undertaken over 10 research projects at or above the provincial and ministerial level, including "The Seventh Five-Year" key project of the National Social Science Fund of China—"Multiple-Volume *Africa*", the major project of the National Social Science Fund of China—"The Compilation and Research on Historical Documents and Oral Historical Materials of China-Africa Relations", "The Seventh Five-Year" research project of the National Education Commission—"History of China-Africa Relations" and "The Tenth Five-Year" Philosophy and Social Science Planning Project of Shanghai—"Studies on Modernization of Developing Countries".

The university began to enroll master's and doctoral students in African History in 1978 and 2003 respectively and has so far fostered over 150 master's and doctoral students. Since 2011, the institute has enrolled African students in History of Africa and Environment Protection. In accordance with the "China-Africa Universities 20+20 Cooperation Plan" of the Ministry of Education, the ECNU and the UDSM jointly foster talents, and the ECNU sends two master's or doctoral students to study in the UDSM every year. The institute cooperates with the Ecole normale supérieure Group and selects students to join the "China-France Joint Program", where China and French jointly foster these doctoral students for African Studies.

The ECNU has established cooperation and exchange relations with overseas universities including the UDSM, the Nelson Mandela African Institutition of Science and Technology in Arusha of Tanzania, Addis Ababa University of Ethiopia, the Ecole normale supérieure in Paris and the Ecole normale supérieure in Lyon of France, and the University of Basel of Switzerland, jointly holding the "Symposium on China-Tanzania Cooperation" and "A Glance at Africa—

Historical Photographs from Namibia and Royal Art from Benin". They also receive and send teachers and students to each other to conduct academic exchanges.

The Institute of African Studies at East China Normal University aims to develop into an important research center and talent fostering center in China for studies on Africa history, African education and African coastal protection.

II. Contact Information

Website: http: //history.ecnu.edu.cn/af

Contact Person: Mu Tao; Email: mutao63@163.com

Correspondence Address: Institute of African Studies, East China Normal University, No. 500 Dongchuan Road, Shanghai, P. R. China.

Center for African Studies, Shanghai Normal University

I. Introduction

The Center for African Studies at Shanghai Normal University, established in 1998, was selected into the list of Regional and Country-Specific Studies Centers Registered with the Ministry of Education in 2011, and was listed in the "China-Africa Think Tanks 10+10 Partnership Plan" by the Ministry of Foreign Affairs in 2014.

The center was founded by Professor ShuYunguo, consultant of the Chinese Society of African Historical Studies and well-known expert on African research in China. The center currently has six full-time researchers, three special researchers and six part-time researchers.

For a long time, the center has been committed to the study of African history, African economy, and China-Africa relations. It has successively completed a number of projects sponsored by the National Social Science Fund of China, the Ministry of Education, Shanghai Philosophy and Social Science Planning Project, and Shanghai Municipal Education Commission. As of the end of 2019, one major project and one general project of the National Social Science Fund of China are in progress.

The center has published more than 10 monographs and more than 100 papers. Since 2012, Professor Zhang Zhongxiang, Professor ShuYunguo and Associate Professor Lin Weicai have published *Studies of the Forum on China-Africa Cooperation, The History of 20th Century African Economy, The History of Pan-Africanism,* and *Voice of African Walkers: The Historical Value Utilization of Records of the British's Travel and Life in Africa in the 19th Century*, all of which are pioneering in China. Integrating project platforms and the center's research characteristics, the center has edited and published a series of translations of *African Economic History* and *Biography of African Historical Figures*. By the end of 2019, the center had published one translated monograph on African economic history and two translated monographs on the biography of African historic figures.

The center pays great attention to its professional characteristics and actively offers advice for China-Africa cooperation and local foreign affairs. It has completed a number of projects of the "China-Africa Joint Research and Exchange Program" of the Ministry of Foreign Affairs and provided multiple consultancy reports for government departments. It attaches great importance to the development of China-Africa relations, disseminating African knowledge and promoting China-Africa relations through publications in newspapers and other media and public lectures. The center puts much emphasis on the characteristics of African economic research. Since the first publication of *Africa's Economy Review* in 2012, it has become one of the major fronts for African economic research in China.

In the context of the booming development of China-Africa exchanges at all levels, in response to the current internationalization of education and academic research, and in view of the characteristic of African studies focusing on field investigations, the center pays much attention to international exchanges, holds international conferences and workshops every year, and invites foreign scholars to the center for academic exchanges and public lectures. All the researchers in the center have visited Africa multiple times and a number of postgraduates have also visited and studied in Africa sponsored by various China-Africa exchange programs of the China Scholarship Council, the Ministry of Foreign Affairs and the Ministry of Education.

The center has always been at the forefront of international academic research and provided constructive suggestions for the long-term development of China-Africa relations. It has established academic and personnel exchanges with the University of Botswana, the University of Nairobi, the University of Zambia, the University of Zimbabwe, as well as some universities and research institutions in South Africa, Nigeria, Benin, Kenya and Zimbabwe. It also maintains close contact with researchers of African studies in Britain, France, America and other countries.

II. Contact Information

Website: http://shcas. shnu.edu.cn/

Contact Person: Liu Weicai; Tel: +86-21-64324535; Email: liuweicai@shnu.edu.cn

Correspondence Address: Center for African Studies, Shanghai Normal University, No. 100 Guilin Road, Shanghai, P. R. China.

Center for West Asian and African Studies, Shanghai Institutes for International Studies

I. Introduction

The Center for West Asian and African Studies at Shanghai Institutes for International Studies, formerly known as the Center of Middle East Studies, was established in 2008. It mainly conducts studies on politics and international relations in the Middle East, energy security and geopolitics, Islamic culture in international politics, China-Middle East relations, international relations in Africa, peace and security in Africa, China-Africa relations, comparative studies on diplomatic policies of major countries to Africa, and others.

The center currently has 10 full-time scientific researchers, including two researchers on African studies. Focusing on China-Africa relations, the Africa research team mainly studies African political security, economy and debt issues, comparison of diplomatic policies of major countries to Africa, and others. The team has published works or translations such as *Is "Africa's Century" Coming? African Ownership and China-Africa Cooperation* and *An Introduction to African Politics*. Its research results have been presented in well-known domestic journals such as *West Asia and Africa, World Economics and Politics, Foreign Affairs Review* and *Contemporary Asia Pacific Studies.* The research team has undertaken a number of projects sponsored by the National Social Science Fund of China, the Ministry of Finance, the Ministry of Foreign Affairs, the Ministry of Education, the Export-Import Bank of China, and China-Africa Joint Research Exchange Program. These relevant research achievements have played an important role in consultancy and application, receiving positive responses among the public.

Based on Shanghai Institutes for International Studies, the Africa research team of the center values international exchanges and cooperation greatly. The institute keeps long-term exchanges and cooperation with more than 10 African institutions, including the Policy Center for the New South in Morocco, the African Policy Institute, the South African Institute of International Affairs, the Center for Chinese Research of Stellenbosch University, and Zimbabwe Economics Society. The team members have been to at least 20 African countries for visits, investigations and exchanges. Meanwhile, the Africa team has received over 10 African visiting scholars in Shanghai.

II. Contact Information

Website: http://www.siis.org.cn/

Wechat Official Account: SIIS1960

Contact Person: Zhou Yuyuan; Email: zhouyuyuan@siis.org.cn

Correspondence Address: No. 15 Lane 195, Tianlin Road, Xuhui District, Shanghai (200233), P. R. China.

Center for East African Studies, Shanghai International Studies University

I. Introduction

With the establishment of Swahili as an undergraduate major, Shanghai International Studies University formally established the Center for East African Studies on May 12, 2019. The center, which is mainly composed of the members of the new major, aims to provide more local texts from a local perspective of East Africa for domestic scholars to conduct social and humanistic investigations and research in East Africa through Swahili studies and with the international teaching platform of Shanghai International Studies University.

The center now has three permanent members, including two professional Swahili teachers of Shanghai International Studies University and one foreign expert sent by the Africa Studies Center of the University of Bayreuth of Germany. The center mainly conducts studies on Swahili literature and East African culture, and all the work is in its initial stage. In addition, the center also cooperates actively with the Publicity Department of the university to edit and translate East African news for the setting up of a multi-language website. As volunteers, students majoring in Swahili also make great contributions to its daily operation. Meanwhile, the center has always been committed to offering consultancy services for the society in the fields of humanities and cultural studies of East Africa, truly putting what they have learned into practice.

In terms of international exchanges, the center actively participates in international academic exchanges, including the Annual Conference of Africa Studies at the University of Bayreuth and the Annual Symposium of the Consortium for Asian and African Studies, and publishes papers every year. Meanwhile, it invites international distinguished scholars to the university to give academic lectures and attend academic meetings. The members of the center graduated from different renowned universities in Africa, Europe and Asia, which ensures that the center could maintain high-level international exchanges.

In the future, the center will keep focusing on literary and cultural research, observe the social development and changes in East Africa from a humanistic perspective, and provide multi-dimensional and deeper reflection and research for Africa studies in China.

II. Contact Information

Contact Person: Ma Yan; Tel: +86-21-67701240

Email: sisumajun@163.com/majun@shisu.edu.cn

Correspondence Address: Room 120, Teaching Building 7, No. 1550 Wenxiang Road, Songjiang District, Shanghai, P. R. China.

Center for African Studies, Institute of Global Studies, SHU

I. Introduction

Founded in February 2018, the Center for African Studies under the Institute of Global Studies at Shanghai University (SHU) aims to build an international high-level academic platform for African regional and country-specific research as well as talent fostering under the new situation of the 21st century. Since its establishment, the center has, on the basis of scientific research platforms and faculty strengths of the Institute of Global Studies, the College of Liberal Arts, and the School of Sociology and Political Science of SHU, and by virtue of the advantages and characteristics of SHU in the disciplinary development of world history, political science and sociology, focused on specific research topics such as China-Africa economic and trade relations, China-Africa medical cooperation, and the operation of Chinese enterprises in Africa, and made satisfactory achievements in teaching, scientific research, policy advisory and talent fostering, laying a good foundation for its development into a high-level, comprehensive, multi-disciplinary research center with important influence at home and abroad in the future. At present, the center is focusing on the following four areas of work.

The center attaches importance to the introduction of high-end talents. In 2018, the center hired Researcher Yang Guang, former director of the Institute of West Asian and African Studies of the Chinese Academy of Social Sciences, executive vice president of China Society for African Studies, and vice president of the Chinese Society of Asian and African Studies. Since 2019, the center has continuously hired young teachers from high-level universities at home and abroad to enrich their scientific research strength.

The center follows the highly internationalized concept of SHU in scientific research and school operation, and makes full use of the existing platform for international enrollment and talent fostering of SHU to carry out teaching practices. The College of Liberal Arts at SHU has trained African students in China for a long time and in large number, and has been rated by the Ministry of Education as a demonstration base for the training of overseas students in China. The Center for African Studies has taken full advantage of it. Up till today, its research and teaching faculty have fostered a dozen of international students from more than 10 African countries, including Ghana, Tanzania and Ethiopia.

The center attaches importance to participating in and establishing long-term international academic exchanges and cooperation. It has signed long-term cooperation agreements with high-level universities in Africa such as the University of Johannesburg in South Africa, and established various academic exchanges with high-level overseas universities of African studies such as the SOAS University of London.

Since its establishment in 2018, the center has held various academic events regularly each year, with its members participating in various research activities of the Department of Historical Studies under the College of Liberal Arts as well as the School of Sociology and Political Science. Since 2019, members of the center have participated in the research at the Institute of Economic Sociology and Multinationals (IESM) at Shanghai University. The Center for African Studies and the Center for Latin American Studies, which is also under the Institute of Global Studies, have carried out research on the theme of "China and the Third World", and the work is progressing smoothly. In addition, members of the center are working actively to undertake various research projects, including the project of the National Social Science Fund of China and the regional and country-specific research project of the Ministry of Education.

II. Contact Information

Website: https://igs.shu.edu.cn

Contact Person: Jiang Huajie; Email: jhj1984@vip.sina.com

Correspondence Address: Institute of Global Studies, Shanghai University, No. 99 Shangda Road, Baoshan District, Shanghai (200444), P. R. China.

Center for African Union Studies, Tianjin University of Technology and Education

I. Introduction

Tianjin University of Technology and Education is one of the first of its kind established in China and one of the first bases for overseas educational aid authorized by the Ministry of Education. In recent years, the university has actively participated in China's educational aid to and cooperation with Africa, sent more than 200 foreign-aid teachers, and trained more than 20, 000 local teachers and students. It has organized various vocational education and training programs for over 1,100 students in over 60 countries. For a long time, the university has maintained close cooperation and exchanges with the African Union (AU) and Ethiopia and signed a Memorandum of Cooperation with the African Union Commission. Entrusted by the Ministry of Education, it has participated in the establishment of the Federal Technical and Vocational Education and Training Institute (FTVETI) of Ethiopia and set up two Confucius Institutes in the institute and Addis Ababa University. It has also undertaken the construction of Lu Ban Workshop in Ethiopia.

In June 2012, in order to meet the national needs for cooperation with Africa and promote the development of the university's educational cooperation with Africa, Tianjin University of Technology and Education set up the Center for African Union Studies based on the previous African Vocational Education

Research Center (founded in 2005). The center is dedicated to research on the AU and particularly Ethiopia in politics, economy, education and other fields. The center's purpose is to carry out country-specific studies on the AU and particularly Ethiopia on the basis of the university's disciplinary characteristics and advantages of educational cooperation with Africa, and promote China's cooperation with the AU and Ethiopia through high-level research results so as to serve the implementation of the "Belt and Road" Initiative.

The center focuses its research on the AU and particularly Ethiopia with a clear objective and systematic planning in scientific research. The major research directions of the center include the legislation, decision-making and operation mechanism of the AU, the relationships between the AU and the outside world, the relationships between the AU and African regional powers, peace and security of the AU and Africa, and the AU and African integration. The main research directions of the center on Ethiopia include Ethiopian politics and economy, education and culture, history, language and literature, and China-Ethiopia relations. Since its establishment, the center has consistently held large academic meetings regularly in the studies of the AU and particularly Ethiopia, actively undertaken research projects from national ministries and commissions including the Ministry of Foreign Affairs, the Ministry of Education, and the Ministry of Culture, and offered suggestions. The center has published *China-Africa Cooperation in the Integration of Africa*, *Made in Africa: Industrial Policy in Ethiopia*, *International Symposium on China-Africa Educational Exchange and Industrial Capacity Cooperation*, and *Ethiopia Education Handbook*, producing certain academic influence in related fields. In June 2017, the Center for African Union Studies was formally included in the list of Regional and Country-Specific Studies Centers Registered with the Ministry of Education.

At present, the center has six full-time researchers. In 2020, the center plans to introduce two high-level experts to further expand its research team. Relying on its advantage in foreign aid in education, the center has invited teachers working overseas from the School of Foreign Language, the School of Economics and Management and the School of Vocational Education of the university as part-time researchers to give full play to their resources and professional advantages to develop multidisciplinary comprehensive research. In addition, the center has also hired Mr. Xie Xiaoyan, former Chinese ambassador to Ethiopia as the honorary director of the center, Ambassador Kuang Weilin, former head of the Chinese Mission to the AU as the center's senior advisor, and Professor Gebre Yntiso, president of Jinka University of Ethiopia, and Professor Tessaye Tafesse, director of the Center for Africa Studies at Addis Ababa University, as guest professors. Besides the full-time and part-time researchers, the center has also established an expert committee composed of well-known African research experts at home and abroad to provide social resources and intellectual support for research projects and the development and decision-making of the center. The members include Professor Admasu Tsegaye, former president of Addis Ababa University in Ethiopia, Professor Li Anshan, chairman of the Chinese Society of African Historical Studies, Mr. Shu Yunguo of the Center for African Studies at Shanghai Normal University, Professor Zhang Xiang of Nankai University, as well as other famous experts and scholars in the field of Africa research in China.

The center has maintained long-term close cooperative relations with the African Union Commission and African universities and think tanks. It signed a Memorandum of Cooperation with the African Union Commission in 2015 and is committed to long-term cooperation in the fields of vocational education, cultural exchanges, joint research and other fields. Since 2014, the center has held educational and cultural seminars for young officials of the AU for many years. In 2017, the center and the AU co-hosted the "International Symposium on China-Africa Educational Exchange and Industrial Capacity Cooperation" in Tianjin. Besides, the center also maintains close academic exchanges and scientific cooperation with multiple research institutes (such as the Center for Africa Research of Addis Ababa University, Ethiopia Research Institute and Ethiopia

Development Research Institute) of some universities, including Addis Ababa University of Ethiopia, Bahir Dar University, and Jinka University.

II. Contact Information

Website: https://caus.tute.edu.cn

Contact Person: Zhai Fengjie; Tel: +86-22-88287970; Email: zhaifengjie@aliyun.com

Correspondence Address: Center for African Union Studies, Tianjin University of Technology and Education, No. 1310 Dagu South Road, Hexi District, Tianjin (300222), P. R. China.

Center for African Studies, Yunnan University

I. Introduction

African studies in Yunnan University enjoy a long history. As early as the 1950s, Yunnan University already began teaching and research on Africa and the Middle East led by Professor Na Zhong, a renowned Yunnan-born Arabic langnage scholar. Professor Na Zhong also served as the first president of the Chinese Society of African Historical Studies, which was founded in 1980. In the 1980s, Professor Zhao Ruifang and Professor Wu Jide of Yunnan University participated in the preparation of the Chinese Society of African Historical Studies and the compilation of the three-volume *Africa*. In 1991, Professor Liu Hongwu returned from studying in Nigeria and formally established a new field of African studies at Yunnan University. He began to recruit graduate students of African studies in 1996 and doctoral students of African studies in 2000. With the official approval of the university, the Center for Asian and African Studies was established in 1998 and the Center for African Studies was established in 2007 with Professor Liu Hongwu as the founding director of the center. With the Center for African Studies as the academic support, Yunnan University became one of the bases for overseas educational aid of the Ministry of Education in 2010, and a project unit of the "China-Africa Joint Research and Exchange Plan" of the Ministry of Foreign Affairs in 2011, a Chinese think tank of the "China-Africa Think Tanks 10+10 Partnership Plan" in 2013, and a Regional and Country-Specific Studies Center Registered with the Ministry of Education in 2017. In March 2017, the Research Center for China-South Africa People-to-people Exchanges of the Ministry of Education was formally launched at Yunnan University.

Professor Liu Hongwu has long served as the chairman of the Academic Committee of the center, and Professor Zhang Yonghong once served as the director. Since October 2019, Professor He Jian has acted as the director, with Deputy Researcher Liang Yijian and Dr. Yang Hui as the deputy directors. At present, the center has 10 full-time researchers (Zhang Yonghong, Zhang Chun, He Jian, Lu Lingyu, Liang Yijian, Wang Tao, Li Xiangyun, Xia Yan, Zhang Jiamei and Yang Hui), eight part-time researchers (Li Zehua, Liu Jun, Ma Yankun, Zhou Qian, Zhao Shulan, Lin Quanxi, Zhao Xian and Li Hongxiang), one postdoctoral research fellow, 12 doctoral students and 20 graduate students.

After decades of accumulated development, the center has gradually developed its own characteristics in the field of African studies in China. Firstly, Yunnan University, qualified to recruit master's students, doctoral students, and post-doctoral fellows, is one of the important institutions to train high-level talents for China's African studies and has so far sent nearly 100 doctoral and master's students of African studies to universities, research institutions and government departments, and some of them have become influential scholars in China. Secondly, it carries out research from the cultural perspective, and especially focuses on the cultural identity in the development process of emerging Africa states. Thirdly, it has long focused on the studies of African country-specific history and special-theme history, and the exploration of special significance of China-Africa relations in the context of dialogue among world civilizations in the light of the development practice of contemporary China-Africa relations. Fourthly, it conducts research on indigenous knowledge, ethnicity, development, environment, poverty reduction, terrorism, and security in Africa on the basis of

Yunnan University's research advantages in cultural diversity and biodiversity. Fifthly, the center adapts to the needs of the times and actively pursues and expands new research directions. After Zhang Chun, He Jian and other researchers joined the center, the topics of African security, diplomacy, law, and ocean and the "Belt and Road" Initiative have been new research directions.

As an academic support institution of education aid base of the Ministry of Education, a regional and country-specific research base of the Ministry of Education, a research center for China-South Africa people-to-people exchanges of the Ministry of Education, a Chinese think tank of the "China-Africa Think Tanks 10+10 Partnership Plan" of the Ministry of Foreign Affairs, and a major platform for the construction of the first-class discipline of Political Science at Yunnan University, the center relies on the profound humanistic heritage of the university and talent advantages in international studies, and maintains extensive cooperation and exchanges with relevant universities and foreign research institutions in African countries, the United States, Japan and European countries in the areas of academic research, scientific cooperation, cultural exchanges and talent fostering.

In recent years, the researchers at the center have undertaken dozens of national and provincial research projects, published more than 10 monographs and over 100 papers of African studies, and have become increasingly prominent in academic circles at home and abroad. The goal of the center in the next few years is to develop into an internationally renowned and domestic first-class research center for African studies in China.

II. Contact Information

Website: http://www.cas.ynu.edu.cn/

Contact Person: Liang Yijian; Tel: +86-871-65039175; Fax: +86-871-65033776

Email: liangyijian1979@163.com

Correspondence Address: Level 3, Yingqiu Hall, Center for African Studies, Yunnan University, No. 2 Cuihu North Road, Kunming City, Yunnan Province (650091), P. R. China.

Institute of African Geography and Resources Environment, Yunnan Normal University

I. Introduction

At the beginning of the 21st Century, Yunnan Normal University began to conduct research on Africa, and gradually developed a research team with Professor Zhou Qian and Dr. Hu Yang as the core. The research team has made certain achievements in the studies of history and culture, resources environment and agrarian system of Kenya and the Democratic Republic of the Congo.

On October 29, 2018, in order to strengthen the construction of the first-level discipline doctoral program of Geography and the first-class discipline of Geography, Yunnan Normal University invited Professor Liu Hongwu, distinguished professor of the Chang Jiang Scholars Program of the Ministry of Education and director of the Institute of African Studies at Zhejiang Normal University, to pay a visit. Professor Liu Hongwu held that Yunnan Normal University boasts a good foundation for constructing the first-level discipline doctoral program of Geography, and that African Geography, as an emerging discipline, enjoys promising prospects. He also gave some suggestions for the university to actively conduct research on African geography.

On January 2, 2019, Yunnan Normal University formally established the Institute of African Geography and Resources Environment relying on the first-level discipline doctoral program of Geography of the university. On December 23, 2019, the unveiling ceremony of the institute was held and Professor Liu Hongwu was hired to be the founding director. Mr. Gert Johannes Grobler, former ambassador of South Africa, Dr. Diallo Yoro, former counsellor of Mali, and Dr. Jin Bo, senior geologist from China National Oil and Gas Exploration and Development Co., Ltd. were invited as special advisors of the institute. Thus a research team combing full-time and part-time researchers was set up to promote its development.

The institute has constantly taken disciplinary construction as the core, think tank service as the function, media communication as the tool, field research in Africa as the prerequisite, and China-Africa cooperation as the approach. Relying on the first-level discipline doctoral program of Geography of the university, it has set up a professional research team to study African geography, resources, environment, and China-Africa cooperation. The research features of the institute are reflected in following aspects: (1) Combining discipline advantages to develop new directions in geography research. Taking advantages of the university's research platforms, talent teams, and technical means, the institute actively draws on the experience of the rapid and successful development of domestic research institutions to gather and cultivate researchers in teams and strengthen the characteristic discipline of "African Geography and Resources Environment". (2) Serving the local and national development strategy and enriching the content of regional and country-specific studies through studies of African geography. The institute pays attention to collecting and analyzing the basic information of African topography, climate, transportation, and resources to enhance the understanding of relevant geographic information in African regional and country-specific studies. (3) Extending the value chain of the discipline and giving full play to the global governance function of geography. Based on geographical research, the institute expands the African research system and promotes African geographic research in other schools and research institutions of Yunnan Normal University. The university has established the Translation Center for African Geographical Research in the School of Foreign Languages and Literature, the Research Center for African History and Geography in the School of History and Administration, and the Research Center for African Resources Development and Law in the School of Politics and Law to serve the "Belt and Road" Initiative.

The institute has three research units, namely, the Institute for African Human and Economic Geography Studies, the Laboratory of Database of African Resources Environment and National Census and Monitoring, and the Institute for African Economy and China-Africa Cooperation. It has 10 full-time researchers (four professors, two associate professors and four lecturers) and 10 part-time researchers, including two foreign researchers.

In the Institute of African Geography and Resources Environment, three professors are recruiting master's, doctoral and post-doctoral candidates in the field of China-Africa cooperation and African geography, and one professor and two associate professors are recruiting master's candidates. Currently, there are 12 graduate students and three doctoral students (including one Nigerian doctoral student) in the institute.

At present, the institute is working on the following two main tasks. (1) The construction of the Database of African Resources Environment and research teams. It mainly takes researchers from the Research Center for Southwest China's Opening-up and Borderland Security and teachers from the School of Tourism and Geography as the core to develop teams for African resources environment monitoring and database construction. It conducts research mainly on the monitoring and development of African resources environment and the construction of resources environment database. (2) The compilation of the 10-volume books on African country-specific studies, "African Geography and Resources Environment Series" (Phase I).

II. Contact Information

Website: https://xbzx.ynnu.edu.cn/index.htm (Temporary Website)

Wechat Official Account: gh_328fcaa925fc

Contact Person: Hu Yang; Email: 374800210@qq.com

Correspondence Address: Level 15, Shixun Building, East Campus, Yunnan Normal University, No. 768 Juxian Road, Chenggong District, Kunming City, Yunnan Province (650500), P. R. China.

Institute of African Studies, Zhejiang Normal University

I. Introduction

Under the auspices of the Ministry of Education (MOE) and the Ministry of Foreign Affairs, the Institute of African Studies at Zhejiang Normal University

(IASZNU) was established in 2007. It is the first comprehensive African research institute in Chinese universities and the first academic institution with a distinguished professor of the Chang Jiang Scholars Program specializing in African Studies. The IASZNU has been selected by the MOE as one of the first "Huang Danian-Type Faculty Teams", a Regional and Country-Specific Studies Center Registered with the Ministry of Education, the Research Center for China-South Africa People-to-people Exchanges, and the Chinese member of the "China-Africa Universities 20+20 Cooperation Plan". It has been selected by the Ministry of Foreign Affairs as a consultancy unit of the Advisory Committee for the China-Africa Joint Research and Exchange Plan and one of the Chinese think tanks of the "China-Africa Think Tanks 10+10 Partnership Plan". The institute is also titled by Zhejiang Province a top-ranking discipline of Political Science, a Provincial 2011 Collaborative Innovation Center, and a new key professional think tank. It has been listed in the "Best Regional Research Center (University-affiliated)" of *Global Go To Think Tank Index Report* by the University of Pennsylvania for four consecutive years. It ranked the sixth among the top 15 Think Tanks of Regional Research and International Relations in the 2019 Chinese Think Tank Index (CTTI) and was rated A+ among the top 100 Think Tanks of Chinese Universities in the 2018 CTTI. It was also selected into the List of Key Think Tanks in "*Comprehensive Evaluation AMI Research Report on Chinese Think Tank (2017)*" published by the Chinese Academy of Social Sciences.

Professor Liu Hongwu, distinguished professor of the Chang Jiang Scholars Program, special expert of Zhejiang Province, special guest consultant of the Advisory Committee of Zhejiang Provincial Government, and consultant of the Advisory Committee of Teaching in Higher Education (Political Majors) by the MOE, is the founding director and chief expert. Focusing on major issues and serving national strategy, the IASZNU takes contemporary African development and China-Africa cooperative relations in the new era as major research directions. Holding the spirit of "developing a passion for Africa, maintaining Chinese characteristics and forming global perspective", it takes the lead in advocating and forming the discipline system for African studies with Chinese characteristics, fosters "African experts" in China and "Chinese experts" in Africa, and creates a high-level academic institution and strategic think tank for China-Africa cooperation.

The IASZNU has four research centers: the Center for African Politics and International Relations, the Center for African Educational Studies, the Center for African Historical and Cultural Studies, and the Center for African Economic Studies. Meanwhile, it has multiple special platforms such as the Branch Center for South African Studies, the Center for Nigerian Studies, the Center for Egyptian Studies, the East Africa Regional and Country-Specific Research Center, the Center for Chinese & African Film and Television Studies, the Center for African Anthropology, the Center for Studies of Francophone Countries of Africa, the Center for China-Africa Education Cooperation Studies, the Center for China-Africa Water Civilization Studies, the Professional Database for African Studies, and the Library for African Studies. The institute has also set up some joint research institutions with other schools of the university, including the Translation Center for African Studies, the Center for African Literature Studies, the Center for African Transportation Studies, the Center for African Geographic Environment Studies, the Center for African Science and Technology Studies, the Center for African Law and Social Development Studies, the Center for African Arts Studies, the Center for African Music and Dance Studies, the Center for China-Africa Trade and Economy Studies, the Center for African Sports Studies, the Center for African Confucius Institutes Studies, and the Center for African Language Survey Studies. The establishment of these research institutions with mutual support and individual focus has promoted the formation of a comprehensive discipline structure for African studies in the university.

The IASZNU has an international team of 40 researchers, including two national talents, six provincial and ministerial-level talents, three former ambassadors, and six scholars from Africa. Among them six hold senior titles, 13 hold associate senior titles, and 27 hold doctoral degrees. All the researchers have academic experiences of long or short-term field research in African countries, forming a network of academic resources featuring "first-class contacts, hands-on experience and first-hand materials". The schools in the university have also developed a part-time research team of almost 200 researchers for African studies to conduct interdisciplinary research.

The IASZNU currently has two interdisciplinary doctoral programs, namely, African Education and Social Development and History of China-Africa Relations, the interdisciplinary master program of African Studies, the first-level discipline master's program of Politic Science, and the second-level discipline master's programs of African Education and African History. It plays an active role in fostering professional interdisciplinary talents for China-Africa cooperation. Its achievements won the second prize of Science Research Famous Achievement Awards in Higher Institution (Humanities and Social Sciences) of the MOE in Politics, the second prize of National Teaching Achievement Award, the first prize of Zhejiang Higher Education Teaching Achievement Award, and the first prize of Zhejiang Postgraduate Association Teaching Achievement Award.

Since its establishment, the IASZNU has undertaken one major project of the National Social Science Fund of China, one major research project of the Fund of Humanities and Social Sciences of the MOE, 23 projects of the National Social Science Fund of China (in addition to supporting other schools of the university to be granted with 20 projects of the National Social Science Fund of China), and over 80 projects from national ministries and commissions including the MOE and the Ministry of Foreign Affairs and joint projects with international institutions. It has compiled and published more than 120 monographs, translations and special reports such as *The MOE Report on the Development of Philosophy and Social Sciences—Annual Report on the Development of Africa*, *Book Series of African Studies of Zhejiang Normal University*, *African Studies* and *Annual Report on China-South Africa People-to-people Exchange*. Among them, the monograph *The study of China-Africa Cooperative Relations in New Era* won the second prize of Science Research Famous Achievement Awards in Higher Institution (Humanities and Social Sciences) of the MOE in Politics and the first prize of Outstanding Achievement Award in Philosophy and Social Sciences of Zhejiang Province, and was selected into the Chinese Academic Translation Project of the National Social Science Fund of China. The book *African Studies from Chinese Perspective* is the first monograph in China to discuss the basic issues on African studies. The book series of *China's Reform and Opening-up and Development Practices* have been translated into English and French and published in African countries. The institute has published more than 400 high-quality papers and filmed two documentaries on China-Africa relations—*Africans in Yiwu* and *TAZARA: A Journey without An End*. It has also established the first African Museum in Chinese universities, which has attracted more than 50,000 visitors in 10 years, become a bridge of China-Africa cultural exchanges, and been selected as one of scientific education bases in Zhejiang.

The IASZNU has edited the *Special Issue of Think Tanks* in *African Studies* and submitted more than 80 consultancy reports to national ministries and commissions, some of which have been approved by national leaders and provincial and ministerial leaders or been accepted by the General Office of the CCCPC, the General Office of the State Council, the MOE journal special issue *Higher Education Think Tanks Research*, *Policy Recommendations for Research Office of the State Council*, or *Xinhua News Agency Internal Reference*. The institute was praised for its "reliable, valuable and practical recommendations for the central ministries and commissions". It founded the China-Africa Think Tank Forum and has hosted eight conferences in China, Ethiopia and South Africa. The forum has been incorporated into the FOCAC framework, exerting great influence at home and abroad. The institute has also organized multiple international conferences such as China-Africa Media & Think Tanks Symposium in line with national strategies. It closely follows the major policies and hotspots of China-Africa relations to interpret China's strategies to Africa and helps to lead public opinions and public diplomacy. It publishes interpretational articles and gives media interviews over 100 times a year. During the FOCAC Beijing Summit in

September 2018, China Central Television (CCTV) invited Director Liu Hongwu to interpret President Xi Jinping's important speech on site and guide international public opinions. In November 2018, Zhejiang Provincial Government invited Director Liu Hongwu to give a special report on promoting Zhejiang-Africa cooperation for provincial leaders, providing policy recommendations for the governor and government departments to promote Zhejiang-Africa cooperation strategy planning and policy implementation.

The IASZNU has established cooperative relations with over 30 universities and think tanks in dozens of African countries and gathered a group of local research partners in Africa. In 2018, the South Africa Branch of the IASZNU was established, which is a significant move towards the Africanization of the institute. It has sent more than 250 teachers and students to Africa for study, research, visits and lectures. The institute has received over 500 dignitaries, scholars, officials and graduate students from Africa, Europe and America, such as former President Benjamin William Mkapa of Tanzania, former President Jerry Rollins of Ghana, and the then Prime Minister Aires Bonifacio Baptista Ali of Mozambique to visit, give lectures and conduct exchanges.

In its long-term creative and pioneering practice, the IASZNU has summarized a "Five in One" disciplinary construction model of "discipline construction as the core, think tank service as the function, field research in Africa as the prerequisite, media communication as the tool and China-Africa cooperation as the approach". It has influenced similar research institutions in China and helped to create a network of African studies in universities. The IASZNU has been praised by the MOE as "having developed a school of its own" and "being representative, exemplary and worth popularizing". The Ministry of Foreign Affairs praised it as "having effectively promoted the development of African studies and the development of research teams in China, enhanced mutual understanding and cooperation between Chinese and African academic communities, and made positive contributions to people-to-people exchanges between China and Africa."

II. Contact Information

Website: http://ias.zjnu.cn/

WeChat Official Account: IASZJNU

Contact Person: Yang Wenjia; Tel: +86-579-82286091; Email: ywj@zjnu.cn

Correspondence Address: Institute of African Studies, Zhejiang Normal University, No. 688 Yingbin Avenue, Wucheng District, Jinhua City, Zhejiang Province (321004), P. R. China.

China-Africa International Business School, Zhejiang Normal University

I. Introduction

The China-Africa International Business School, Zhejiang Normal University, established in November 2010, is the first domestic business school dedicated to the promotion of China-Africa economic and trade cooperation. The school hires Mr. Liu Guijin, the first special representative of the Chinese government on African Affairs and former ambassador of China to Zimbabwe and South Africa, as its founding director. In April 2014, the school was integrated with the School of Economics and Management and began the operation mode of "one faculty for two schools". It is characterized by economics, trade and business administration, and is dedicated to fostering of African experts on China and Chinese experts on Africa. It strives to form an educational system integrating talent fostering, personnel training, business consultancy and academic research so as to promote China-Africa cooperation in various fields including economy, trade, education, and human resource development.

The school offers 10 majors for undergraduate students. Among them, international economics and trade is a provincial-level fostering major for internationalization, e-commerce is a provincial-level outstanding major, financial management and business management are provincial-level key majors to be fostered, and e-commerce and financial management are university-level internationalization majors. The school also has professional master's degree programs in international business management and Master of Business Administration (MBA). It currently has more than 2,400 full-time students, including more than 460 postgraduates and nearly 500 overseas students. In order to strengthen Chinese students' understanding of the African market, it has set up Africa-related courses such as "Introduction to Africa", "China-Africa Economic and Trade Relations", "African Trade and Investment", and "African Commercial Law". Since 2013, over ten outstanding Chinese undergraduates have been selected each year as exchange students to the University of Stellenbosch in South Africa.

As to the fostering of overseas students, about 2/3 of them come from Africa. Since 2017, the school has organized one Touchroad IMBA class each for the governments of Lesotho and Botswana in a pilot model of school-government-enterprise collaborative fostering. In 2016, the school sent overseas students to participate in the China College Students' Entrepreneurship Competition for the first time, and won the silver award in the MBA Special Event. In 2019, African students of the school won the gold medal in the Zhejiang College Students' "Internet Plus" Innovation and Entrepreneurship Competition. In August 2020, African students of the school won three gold awards in the 6th China International College Students' "Internet+" Innovation and Entrepreneurship Competition.

In order to further promote the research in China-Africa economic and trade relations, the school has established a few institutions specializing in this field, including the "China-Africa International Business Talent Training Platform" under the Department of Commerce of Zhejiang Province, the "Institute for Transnational Operation of Chinese and African Enterprises" and the "Center for China-Africa Economic and Trade Relations" set up by the school, and the "China Zionlion International Business Institute" jointly established with related enterprise. The school attaches great importance to the studies of China-Africa economic and trade relations. Up till today, the teachers of the school have undertaken and completed eight national projects and 14 provincial and ministerial projects. Another 12 national projects and 10 provincial and ministerial projects are in progress. Relevant achievements have won two first prizes and one third prize of Zhejiang Provincial Philosophy and Social Science Outstanding Achievement Award. Since 2016, the school has published the *Development Report on Zhejiang-Africa Industrial Capacity Cooperation* and the *Development Report on China-Africa Industrial Capacity Cooperation* for four consecutive years, and has successively published the book series of *Studies of China-Africa Economic and Trade Relations* and translated books including *African Economy and Trade*.

The school encourages teachers to actively conduct research in African countries. At present, more than 20 teachers are engaged in the studies of China-Africa economic and trade development. In the past five years, more than 10 teachers have been to universities in South Africa, Kenya, Nigeria, Ethiopia and other African countries for academic visits or field investigations.

The research team of China-Africa economic and trade relations actively provides advisory services for the decision-making of the government. In March 2019, at the Symposium on Zhejiang's Economic and Trade Cooperation with Africa, the Department of Commerce of Zhejiang Province issued the *Action Plan of Zhejiang Province to Enhance Economic and Trade Cooperation with Africa* (2019-2022) compiled with the participation of the teachers from the school. In September 2020, a group of teachers from the school participated in the formulation of the *Fourteenth Five-Year Plan for Zhejiang's Exchanges and Cooperation with Africa*. Focusing on the actual needs of China-Africa business and investment, the school is developing the "Cooperative Service Platform for China-Africa Business and Investment" so as to build a "one-stop" service platform for communication and management of China-Africa business and investment and provide specialized advisory services for investment in Africa.

The school actively organizes large-scale forums to expand its social influence. Since 2015, the school has held six consecutive sessions of the Forum on China-Africa Economic and Trade Relations in cooperation with the Jinhua Municipal

Government, with 2,000 participants from government departments at all levels as well as academic and business circles. Nearly 400 enterprises within and outside the province and from African countries benefitted from these forums. Meanwhile, the school successfully held two sessions of the Forum on China-South Africa Youth Innovation and Entrepreneurship, with Yuan Jiajun, the then governor of Zhejiang Province, present at the second Forum on China-South Africa Youth Innovation and Entrepreneurship held in South Africa.

II. Contact Information

Website: http://sxy.zjnu.edu.cn/main.htm; WeChat Official Account: zsdjg_2012

Contact Person: Huang Yupei; Tel: +86-579-82298567; Email: yupeihuang@zjnu.edu.cn

Correspondence Address: China-Africa International Business School, Zhejiang Normal University, No. 688 Yingbin Avenue, Jinhua City, Zhejiang Province (321004), P. R. China.

Center for China-Africa Agriculture and Forestry Research, Zhejiang A&F University

I. Introduction

The Center for China-Africa Agriculture and Forestry Research (CAFOR) was jointly established in Hangzhou by Zhejiang A&F University (ZAFU) and the International Network for Bamboo and Rattan (INBAR) in December 2012. It aims to, through cooperation with African partners, build a platform of cooperation in education, science and technology for joint scientific research and capacity building on the development of African agriculture and forestry; and through South-South cooperation, promote China-Africa cooperation and exchanges in agriculture, forestry and related fields and boost sustainable development of agriculture and forestry in China and Africa.

Relying on its natural resources in agriculture, forestry and other aspects, the center conducts education, research and consultancy in all aspects and from multiple dimensions, with particular advantages in bamboo, tea and cultural research. Through studying the development of African agriculture and forestry, it explores effective models for China-Africa cooperation in the technology of agriculture and forestry. Through scientific and technological cooperation and cultural exchanges with Africa, it promotes the transfer and dissemination of agricultural and forestry knowledge and technology, improves the level of scientific research and technological cooperation, and promotes sustainable development of agriculture and forestry in China and Africa. Based on ZAFU, the center draws on the experience of other educational and scientific research institutes in China as well as that of the INBAR to explore effective models of cooperation and talent fostering in agricultural and forestry science and technology. Meanwhile, it implements various strategic cooperation projects through the worldwide network of member countries and partners of the INBAR to provide technological and policy consultancy services on agricultural and forestry cooperation and win-win development between China and African countries. By promoting South-South cooperation, it satisfies the development needs of China and African countries. By promoting research and developing the potential of characteristic agricultural and forestry resources like bamboos, it contributes to food security, environmental protection and poverty eradication in China and African countries.

The center mainly develops towards the following four goals: (1) establishing a research and consultancy institute on China-Africa agricultural and forestry development under the framework of South-South cooperation to better serve the needs of the Chinese government in cooperating with foreign countries (especially those in Africa); (2) establishing an institute of scientific and technological support for the development of Africa's agriculture and forestry to promote effective application of knowledge and technology of ZAFU and the INBAR in South-South cooperation; (3) establishing a platform of higher education and capacity building in African agricultural and forestry to foster high-level and international agricultural and forestry researchers for China and African countries; and (4) establishing a platform of informational and technological dissemination for China-Africa cooperation and development in green economy so as to study and publish papers, research reports, consultancy reports and monographs on the development of African agriculture and forestry and enhance the academic capacity and international influence of the INBAR and ZAFU.

The center is headed by Lou Yiping and currently has six researchers and four guest professors. Under the center are three institutes: the Institute of Agriculture and Environment, the Institute of Forestry and Climate Change, and the Institute of Sustainable Consumption and Production and Food Security. In addition, the center has an executive office for daily personnel, financial and other administrative work; and a Department of Development and Exchanges responsible for external liaison, publicity and fund-raising.

The center has carried out preliminary research in a total of 16 research and demonstration projects in the following five major directions and fields: African agricultural resources, the demonstration effect of China's agricultural aid to Africa, the formulation of strategies for the development of agricultural industries in African countries, the response of African forestry to climate changes, and the capacity building of agriculture and forestry in the "Belt and Road" countries, receiving a total funding of about 19 million yuan. In the past five years, it has published four monographs of research on Africa, more than 20 research papers, and 10 special research reports; and organized nine large-scale international trainings and five domestic trainings, attracting more than 400 trainees from 17 countries in three continents, especially those from the "Belt and Road" countries and African countries.

The center has established substantive project links with more than 10 domestic and foreign government departments and international organizations including the Ministry of Agriculture, the Ministry of Commerce, the European Union, the Citibank Foundation, and the Food and Agriculture Organization of the United Nations; and has designed strategic plans for agricultural and forestry crops and products for Kenya, Cameroon, Rwanda, Vietnam and other countries.

The center participated in the projects of "Research on the Methodology of Carbon Sequestration in Chinese Bamboo Forests" and "Promotion and Application of Bamboo Forest Carbon Sequestration Methodology in Africa". It also carried out carbon sequestration demonstrations in Kenya and Ethiopia, promoting the implementation of China's climate strategy of South-South cooperation. The projects helped a master project of the university "Key Technologies and Applications of Carbon Sink Monitoring, Sink Enhancement and Emission Reduction in the Bamboo Forest Ecosystem" win the second prize of the 2017 National Science and Technology Progress Award.

II. Contact Information

Website: http://cafor.zafu.edu.cn

Contact Person: Yang Guangsheng; Tel: +86-571-63746816; Email: gsyang@zafu.edu.cn

Correspondence Address: Room 616, Laboratory Building, Zhejiang A&F University (Yijin Campus), No. 252 Yijin Street, Lin'an District, Hangzhou City, Zhejiang Province, P. R. China.

Research Center for African Law and Social Development, Zhejiang Normal University

I. Introduction

The Research Center for African Law and Social Development at Zhejiang Normal University (ZJNU) was jointly established by China Law Society and ZJNU in November 2015. It is dedicated to African law research and China-Africa legal cooperation, and aims to develop into a domestic first-class and high-level innovative team that integrates African law research, related personnel fostering, specialist training and social services as well as international legal cooperation with Africa.

Its researchers are mainly composed of teachers from the College of Law and Political Science, Zhejiang Normal University. The team currently has 10 core members, or specifically, two professors, four associate professors and four lecturers. Among them nine have doctoral degrees, six have more than half a year's experience of studying abroad, and eight are under 45 years old. The director of the center is Professor Wu Ka.

From 2016 to 2019, the members of the center visited Kenya, Ethiopia, South Africa, Namibia, Tanzania and other African countries to attend academic conferences and conduct academic exchanges.

The center has established a number of high-level research and innovation platforms, including "Research Center for African Law and Social Development" (established in November 2015 together with China Law Society), "Center for China-Africa Legal Studies" (established in May 2019 together with the University of Dar es Salaam, Tanzania), and "Research Center for Discerning African Law" (a university-funded high-level research and innovation platform incubation project established in June 2019).

In November 2019, the center completed the project "Translation of Tanzanian Legal Texts" commissioned by the Chinese Embassy to Tanzania; and in December of the same year, *The International Legal Guarantee Mechanism of China-Africa Capacity Cooperation* written by the head of the center, Professor Wu Ka, was published.

II. Contact Information

Contact Person: Wu Ka; Email: wuka@163.com

Correspondence Address: Building 45, College of Law and Political Science, Zhejiang Normal University, Jinhua City, Zhejiang Province (321004), P. R. China.

Mingwei Risk Analysis

I. Introduction

With rapid expansion of China's influence in Africa, the pressure and demand for safeguarding interests in Africa are increasing day by day. Under this background, Mingwei Risk Analysis, the first non-governmental think tank for

African studies in China, was established in Hangzhou on December 22, 2015. It was launched by a number of researchers from domestic universities and attracted a group of young scholars engaged in African studies, all of whom have experiences of in-depth field research or visits in Africa. In terms of the research field, the group pays attention to the combination of general studies with country-specific studies, substantially covering all major countries and fields in Africa.

Mingwei Risk Analysis aims to develop into a non-governmental think tank specializing in the study and assessment of African risks, and takes as its own responsibility to promote Chinese research on Africa and provide intellectual support for safeguarding China's interests in Africa. In order to better safeguard China's interests in Africa and establish industry-university-research cooperation, Mingwei Risk Analysis chooses risk assessment, which features urgency, comprehensiveness and inclusiveness, as its key study area. Based on African country-specific studies, it carries out African security risk assessment mainly in political and economic fields, and gradually expands to law, society, culture and other fields.

It conducts organizational construction in the form of a research group which is composed of researchers from universities, students of African studies and enterprise personnel. At the end of 2013, a civil war broke out in South Sudan. The group leader established the South Sudan Research Group and provided intellectual support for Chinese-invested enterprises there and South Sudan-related departments in predicting the development of the situation. In 2015, the group expanded its research field to Sudan and established the Sudan and South Sudan Research Group. With the expansion of the research group as well as its research scope, on May 1, 2017, the Sudan and South Sudan Research Group turned into the East Africa Research Group, which currently has 30 members. Mingwei Risk Analysis holds regular meetings once a month to discuss the African situation of that month and conduct theme discussions and team-building activities.

It also uses its WeChat official account "sinosouthsudan" as a platform to publish its research results. In addition to thematic analysis, it releases the news of the latest situation in East Africa every day. From 2014 to 2019, it kept doing this for six consecutive years, providing a window for the academic and business circles to observe East Africa. In addition, it keeps close ties and cooperation with domestic and foreign institutions of African research, business agencies and personnel in Africa, and Africa-related departments, and regularly writes advisory reports for relevant departments. Since November 2019, it has been releasing the *Daily Briefing of African Top Stories*, which consists of four sections respectively focusing on North Africa, East Africa, West Africa and Southern Africa, and tracks the development of nearly 30 countries, virtually the whole of Africa, with a focus on four regional powers: Nigeria, Egypt, Ethiopia and South Africa, mainly in the fields of politics, economy and diplomacy development of African countries. Based on that, it publishes a monthly collection of African news.

II. Contact Information

Website: http://www.mwara.cn/

WeChat Official Account: sinosouthsudan

Contact Person: Zhou Jun; Email: 329648400@qq.com

Correspondence Address: Room 712, Building C, Pioneering Park of Zhejiang Gongshang University, No. 198 Jiaogong Road, Xihu District, Hangzhou City, Zhejiang Province, P. R. China.

Center for North African Studies, Zhejiang Gongshang University

I. Introduction

In May 2017, Jin Yibin, party committee secretary of the CPC at Zhejiang Gongshang University (ZJSU), led an education delegation to Morocco and Tunisia and discussed cooperation with universities and educational institutions of North Africa, reaching consensus in a series of matters. Afterwards, the Center for North African Studies was established by the School of Foreign Languages of ZJSU in cooperation with domestic and foreign research institutions including the University of Rouen in France, the French Research Center of Wuhan University, the African Francophone Research Center of Wuhan University, the Francophone Research Center of Beijing Foreign Studies University, Alliance française de Hangzhou, Hangzhou Translation Association, China-Africa Bridge and Yxintent. The academic resources of the center came from various schools of ZJSU. Among them were the School of Foreign Languages, the College of International Education, the School of Oriental Languages and Culture, the School of Humanities and Communication, the School of Tourism and Urban-Rural Planning, the MBA School, the School of Economics and the School of Public Administration. In December 2017, the center was approved by the university as a university-level scientific research institute.

The center aims to develop into a comprehensive research institute specializing in the studies of politics, economy, history, culture, language, religion and society of North Africa, gaining greater influence than similar institutes in the whole province and the whole country at large. Specifically, it works to (1) provide think tank consultancy service for the decision-making of the local governments from an academic perspective; and (2) from the perspective of actual needs, serve the local region with its research results to expand the exchanges between Zhejiang Province as well as Hangzhou City and Africa, and provide advisory service for enterprises and institutions to improve and expand their businesses in Africa, meeting the local needs of Zhejiang Province and Hangzhou City.

The research of the center is guided by Xi Jinping Thought on Socialism with Chinese Characteristics for a New Era; problem-oriented; studies macro problems from the perspective of concrete details; focuses on basic, applied and comparative research; and conducts research in such fields as China-Africa relations, France-Africa relations, North African culture, North African foreign relations and North African economy.

The center is directed by Professor Li Dandi, Dean of the School of Foreign Languages. The full-time researchers are mainly teachers of French, Arabic,

English, German, Spanish and other languages from the university. Meanwhile, the center hires well-known scholars from the University of Rouen in France and other institutes as part-time researchers. The center also hires a number of former Chinese diplomats who once worked in the Chinese embassies and consulates in North Africa and accumulated many years of front-line experience in diplomacy as part-time researchers. Also working part-time in the center are researchers and executives from academic institutes including the Chinese Academy of Social Sciences, China Institute of International Studies, Shanghai Institute for International Studies, China Institute of Contemporary International Relations, Wuhan University, Beijing Foreign Studies University, China Foreign Affairs University and the University of International Relations as well as public institutions and social groups including Électricité de France, Zhejiang Construction Investment Group Co., Ltd., Hangzhou E-Business Institute, China-Africa Bridge, China-Africa Economic and Trade Research Institute, Alliance française de Hangzhou, Hangzhou Translation Association and Yxintent. The group enjoys a reasonable age structure and conducts research in various fields.

The center has held multiple seminars, lectures and meetings in the related fields and conducted a series of preliminary research on French policies toward Africa, China-Africa economic and trade exchanges, Chinese companies in Africa, and works by African writers, yielding some achievements. In addition, the center has sent out teachers and students to actively participate in the aid programs for Africa initiated by the Ministry of Commerce and the provincial Department of Commerce, with a number of French-speaking students working in Africa.

The center hires Jean-Marie Cambaceres, former attorney general of Gard, former member of the French Parliament, and president of the France Asia Association, Philippe Lane, former vice-president of the University of Rouen, doctoral supervisor, and famous linguist and diplomat of France, FouedLaroussi, professor of the University of Rouen, and doctoral supervisor, and others as part-time researchers. It also maintains long-term cooperation with Professor Oussama Karoui from Tunisia and Professor Fabien Neibaf from France.

The center has industriously carried out various activities in management and research and is making all efforts to gain official approval upon the expiration of the incubation period so as to make further contributions toward the development of the country and particularly the local region.

II. Contact Information

Website: http://flc.hzic.edu.cn/

Contact Person: Chen Jianwei; Email: cjwp2017@163.com

Correspondence Address: School of Foreign Languages, Zhejiang Gongshang University, No. 18 Xuezheng Street, Xiasha Neighborhood, Hangzhou City, Zhejiang Province (310018), P. R. China.

Research Center for African Coastal Countries, Zhejiang Ocean University

I. Introduction

The Research Center for African Coastal Countries at Zhejiang Ocean University was established in June 2017. Centering on "Marine Africa" and "African Ocean", it mainly studies marine policy, law, economy, industries, science and technology, environmental protection, and culture of African costal countries. It actively promotes a series of cooperation between China and Africa in the maritime matters and works to build a platform for academic, cultural and educational cooperation and exchanges for the establishment of a China-Africa maritime community with a shared future. The director of the center is Professor Yang Guangxi.

Currently, the center conducts studies in such fields as African marine policies and law, marine economy and industries, language and marine culture of African costal countries, education of African coastal countries, and African marine environmental protection and marine technology.

The center actively promotes the education of African students. Batches of postgraduate and undergraduate exchange students from African coastal countries have been enrolled in different majors including marine science, aquaculture, marine food, and Chinese language and literature. It has also signed cooperation agreements with a number of African universities including Rhodes University in South Africa, the University of Dar es Salaam in Tanzania and the Université Libre de Dakar in Senegal.

The center has 20 full-time and part-time researchers, and has undertaken a number of projects in African marine research sponsored by the National Social Science Fund of China, Zhejiang Provincial Social Science Fund, the Ministry of Science and Technology, and Zhejiang Provincial Department of Science and Technology. With gradual development of the research group, research focus and research features, the center has gained some influence in this field. In 2019, the center was approved for one project of the National Social Science Fund of China and one major project of Zhejiang Provincial Social Science Fund, and published one monograph, all of which being in the field of African marine and related research. In addition, four teachers made academic visits to African countries.

II. Contact Information

Contact Person: Yang Guangxi; Email: 1136613228@qq.com

Correspondence Address: School of Humanities and Teacher Education, Zhejiang Ocean University, Zhoushan City, Zhejiang Province (316004), P. R. China.

Center for Studies of the Great Lakes Region of Africa, ZhejiangYuexiu University

I. Introduction

The Center for Studies of the Great Lakes Region of Africa at Zhejiang Yuexiu University of Foreign Languages (ZYUFL) was approved by the Department of International Cooperation and Exchange of the Ministry of Education and established in March 2021. It is a Regional and Country-Specific Studies Center Registered with the Ministry of Education focusing on the Great Lakes region of Africa, and mainly studies politics, economy, history, culture and international relations of the region.

In recent years, Zhejiang Province has carried out frequent economic and trade exchanges with African countries, with the number of enterprises and institutions investing in Africa continuously increasing and the amount of investment gradually rising. The center will, on the basis of exchanges and cooperation between Zhejiang Province and the Great Lakes region of Africa as well as local economic ties and exchanges, focus its work to meet the needs of national development strategies. The center will, in accordance with the spirit of the instructions of the Zhejiang Provincial Government and in conjunction with the cooperation and exchange of framework of the Forum on China-Africa Cooperation, make full use of its platform to provide consultancy on national conditions, culture, information and risk awareness, particularly for Zhejiang enterprises in Africa and Chinese enterprises intending to explore the African market.

The center will, relying on the platform of friendly cooperation established between Zhejiang Province and the Great Lakes region of Africa, and by virtue of good scientific research strength and language advantages of ZYUFL, work actively to build a regional and country-specific research base focusing on the Great Lakes region of Africa, and strive to develop the base into a "state-level research think tank focusing on the Great Lakes region of Africa and featuring clearly-defined orientation, distinctive features, sound mechanism and excellent performance". The center will carry out categorized research on the country, society, politics, economy and culture of the Great Lakes region, so as to develop into a major state-level research center on the Great Lakes region of Africa in the whole province and East China at large, providing consultancy services for government departments and foreign-related enterprises.

The center will monitor political developments in the region over the next five years; provide policy advisories on major practical issues such as China-Africa relations and the national situation of the Great Lakes region; strengthen its capacity in offering practical solutions, predicting the situational development and providing quick response advisories; guide the public opinion; promote think-tank diplomacy; and make efforts to develop into a bridge and link between China and the Great Lakes region of Africa for the development of the bilateral friendship.

The center boasts a team of researchers featuring diverse professional orientation, outstanding research abilities and a reasonable age structure, with Professor Ge Jinling, party secretary of the Euro-Languages College of ZYUFL, as the director, and Professor Liu Chengfu,executive deputy director of China Society for African Affairs, as the executive director. The center hires Professor He Wenping, researcher at the Institute of West-Asian and African Studies of the Chinese Academy of Social Science (China-Africa Institute), and Professor Wang Zhan, director of the African Research Center, which is a Regional and Country-Specific Studies Center Registered with the Ministry of Education, as chief researchers. The center also hires more than 20 experts from within and outside the university, including Professor Li Jianying of Shanghai Normal University as well as Professor Wang Yonglong, dean of the Institute of Modern Economic Management, Yang Xiaoping, dean of the College of International Business, and Lu Haiping, party secretary of the Euro-Languages College, of ZYUFL to form a team of contract researchers and conduct comprehensive, multidisciplinary and cross-field research on the Great Lakes region of Africa.

The center adheres to the principle of “focusing on major issues and serving national strategies”, and focuses on the studies of “contemporary African development issues” and “China-Africa cooperative relations in the new era”, covering the aspects of application research, fundamental research and policy advisories, with corresponding subtopics under each major direction. The application research includes: (1) investigations and studies of the investment, production and operation of Zhejiang businessmen, mainly from the eastern region of Zhejiang, in the Great Lakes region of Africa, as well as their acceptance of and integration into the local culture; and (2) investigations and studies of the public opinion in the countries of the Great Lakes region of Africa about China. The fundamental research includes: (1) country-specific and social studies of the Great Lakes region of Africa; (2) political studies of the countries in the Great Lakes region of Africa; (3) economic studies of the countries in the Great Lakes region of Africa; and (4) studies of the local culture of the countries in the Great Lakes region of Africa. The policy advisory research includes: (1) the study of the social situation in the Great Lakes region of Africa, (2) the risk and security assessment of Chinese investment in the countries of the Great Lakes region of Africa, (3) the study of the political development trend in the countries of the Great Lakes region of Africa in the next five years, and (4) the study of the local culture in the countries of the Great Lakes region of Africa.

II. Contact Information

Contact Person: Shi Jun; Tel: +86-575-89114496

Correspondence Address: Room 230, Tower E, Research Building, Zhejiang Yuexiu University of Foreign Languages, No. 428 Kuaiji Road, Jishan Neighborhood, Yuecheng District, Shaoxing City, Zhejiang Province (312000), P. R. China.